insights
for
leaders
in youth
ministry

99 thoughts
on leading well

Group

Reza Zadeh

99 Thoughts on Leading Well
Insights for Leaders in Youth Ministry

Copyright © 2010 Simply Youth Ministry

group.com
simplyyouthministry.com

Credits
Author: Reza Zadeh
Executive Developer: Nadim Najm
Chief Creative Officer: Joani Schultz
Copy Editor: Rob Cunningham
Cover Art and Production: Veronica Lucas
Production Manager: DeAnne Lear

ISBN 978-0-7644-4315-2

10 9 8 7 6 5 4 3 2 1   18 17 16 15 14 13 12 11 10

Printed in the United States of America.

dedication

There are so many people that helped shape
the way I think about leadership. This book
is dedicated to every football coach, personal
mentor, and pastor who has influenced my life
and the way I view leadership. My wife Allyson
and our beautiful children have inspired and
supported me greatly. Thank you.

table of contents

your inner life

When your life is built upon a solid foundation, your leadership can withstand the storms.

I grew up on the California coast, and it seemed like every year we heard reports of wealthy homes being destroyed by mudslides. Millionaires would build these massive houses on hillsides overlooking the Pacific Ocean, but strong rainstorms threatened these homes because they were not built upon solid enough foundations. The weather weakened the foundations, which couldn't provide enough stability for withstanding storms.

As a leader you will face trials and challenges that will test your leadership. To lead your people and ministry through difficult times, you need a solid foundation for your own life. Foundations are only as strong as they are deep. I encourage you to find ways to build your life upon a solid foundation of prayer, Scripture, and an everyday walk with Jesus. Work on finding out what God declares is true about you as a follower of Jesus.

Studying and obeying the Bible will help you develop a strong biblical foundation for your life—and ultimately for your leadership.

2 Uncertainty doesn't disqualify you from leadership—it qualifies you.

For many years I made the mistake of thinking that uncertainty about the future meant I was a bad leader. But I have spoken to many leaders who told me that the cloudiness of the future did not mean that I was a bad leader—it revealed the need for me to be a strong leader. Every leader and every ministry will face uncertain times. Don't let that scare you—let it encourage you. You are needed!

For a few years, our ministry faced so many challenges and uncertain times that I felt that the church made a big mistake by hiring me and that I needed to step aside and allow God to raise up someone else more qualified. After some great encouraging prayer partners, and many leadership lessons later, I am convinced that I am the person that God has called to lead this particular ministry—and that there are no accidents in God's economy.

Your leadership role is not an accident either. Don't doubt God's plans because of the uncertain times you face as a leader. Take things one step at a time and trust God as you take each step. When you look back, you will see that you were the right person for the job. Have confidence in yourself, but more importantly have confidence in God's sovereignty.

3 Identify your unique mission as a leader.

Two years ago I was challenged by a mentor to write out my "life mission statement." I thought it was a weird thing to do. We have mission statements for our ministries and for our church, but come on—a mission statement for my life? It took me a few weeks to narrow it down, but I can tell you that it has enhanced many areas of my life, especially my ability to lead.

We have mission statements for our ministries and churches so we can evaluate our programs and see if they line up with our overall goal. Having a mission statement for your life can do the same thing. Writing out my life mission statement has allowed me to evaluate all the ways I use my energy as a leader. If a certain opportunity does not line up with my life mission statement, I pass on it. Too many times we let circumstances dictate how we live, and as leaders we find ourselves servicing the next big emergency that arises in our ministries. If we were really able to be mission-minded, then we would be able to live and not just let life happen to us.

To be a focused leader you must learn to eliminate distractions.

A laser and a fluorescent light bulb both emit light rays. So why is one used in surgeries and has the ability to burn your skin, while the other is mostly harmless when we are exposed to it? The reason: A laser is much more focused light. Think of "focus" as eliminating distractions, rather than giving something attention. I believe that as we eliminate the distractions that cloud our thoughts and vision, we give our undivided attention to something worthwhile. Think about all the times you're behind the wheel of your car. You need to remain focused on your driving—but if you're distracted by your cell phone, your fast food, or the three coffee-infused student leaders in the backseat, you're unable to focus as well as you'd like.

It is mentally exhausting to spend your energy giving something your attention. But there is something peaceful about relieving yourself of surrounding distractions. As a leader you must learn to eliminate distractions from your life. If you find yourself continually distracted by certain things, chances are you are not living up to your potential as a strong leader. Find ways to eliminate the distractions in your life. They may be time wasters—or even responsibilities that keep you from doing what's most important as the leader of a ministry. Find these distractions and eliminate them, because as you remove them you will find yourself more and more focused as you serve your ministry.

Nothing breeds leadership like a life of integrity.

The integrity of the honest keeps them on track; the deviousness of crooks brings them to ruin (Proverbs 11:3 The Message). Isn't it interesting how a proverb can seem so simple in principle yet so difficult in practice? Think back to some admired leaders whose private lives have been revealed— and were inconsistent with their public lives. This lack of integrity affected their ministries and the people around them.

If you are reading this book then you probably serve in some sort of leadership role in a church. Some of the people you lead believe you are above mistakes as a leader; people expect their ministry leaders to live faultless lives. You and I know that this isn't possible. Plus, living a life of integrity does not mean living a life of perfection. Having integrity means taking responsibility for your words and actions. Having integrity involves everything from following through on your word to asking forgiveness when you wrong someone.

Release yourself from thinking that a person of integrity lives a perfect, flawless life. A life of integrity is not flawless; it is a life filled with true repentance. You will grow your influence as a leader if you walk humbly and allow your life to align with what you teach. When you fall short of God's glory, it doesn't mean you have failed as a leader, but you do have the opportunity to lead people in how you respond in life.

6 Letting God's Spirit shine through you requires time spent with him.

Have you ever put a marshmallow in a microwave oven? When a marshmallow is exposed to the microwaves, the molecules expand because of the heat, and the marshmallow grows in size. Think of that marshmallow as a representation of the life of God in you, and think of the exposure to microwaves as time spent with the Father. The more time a leader spends with God, the greater the life of God will grow inside that person. And it's only a matter of time before what's growing on the inside starts to expose itself on the surface.

You can't give what you don't have. If you are leading a ministry, how can you expect to lead people spiritually if you are not exposing yourself to the only one who can fill you? Jesus spent time with the Father in solitude, and these times were crucial for him as he ministered to people. Jesus used the illustration of a vine and branches that bear fruit to clarify this principle. Spend time with God in prayer and watch the Lord's marvelous light expose itself through you as you impact people.

7 With an open heart, every situation is an opportunity to grow.

The Christian life is a journey—an expedition we take with God. It is an invitation to walk with God and have him show us ways we can grow personally. As leaders, our journey takes on new significance because we have people following and learning from us. In every situation we come across on this journey, we have the opportunity to learn from God. The Apostle Paul tells us this: *And we know that God causes everything to work together for the good of those who love God and are called according to his purpose for them (Romans 8:28)*. The key is having an open heart to the Holy Spirit revealing spiritual truth as you encounter different situations in life. God is a great tour guide—give him permission to educate you in areas that you need to be educated in and watch him grow you in huge ways.

your inner life

8 Don't try being the Messiah—you're not good at it.

Even though I try, I am not a good Messiah. I have found myself trying to fix things for people and be their savior. Many leaders make this same mistake. It is called a "Messiah Complex"—our attempts to fix everything and essentially play the role of Jesus in the lives of people. As a minister or leader, you probably have a heart for people and don't want to see them struggle through life. You want to help solve problems and provide for people when needed. This is a good thing, and praise God you have this kind of heart for people.

But one of our roles as church leaders is to equip other Christians with the tools necessary to follow Jesus for the rest of their lives. This process includes encouraging people to turn to God for answers in life. You are called to be a minister of the Word, an encourager, and an equipper. You were never called to be the Messiah for the ones that you lead. Release yourself of this pressure and rest in the fact that God has called you to minister. Leave the ultimate provision up to God.

9 Inspire people by what you do, not just by what you say.

Actions speak louder than words. We've all heard this saying at one point in our lives, and as leaders we must adhere to this principle. Like it or not, your life as a leader will sometimes feel like a glass bowl, and your actions will be scrutinized by other people—especially those that you lead. A few years ago NBA star Charles Barkley told the press that he didn't sign up to be a role model and it wasn't fair for him to have his personal life examined in the media. What Sir Charles wouldn't admit was that he was a leader whether he liked it or not. Leadership is influence, and the lives lived by people considered leaders will influence the lives of the people that follow them.

As a minister or leader, your life is an open book, and this open book is teaching other people principles of life. Develop a lifestyle that integrates your faith into every area of life. You can talk about spiritual principles all you want in conversations with people, in your Facebook™ status updates, and from the pulpit, but if you aren't living out what you are saying, then your influence will be greatly diminished. Lead your ministry by the way you live. Pursue a life of integrity and let your actions line up with what you teach.

Spiritual leadership involves the same fear that rock climbers have—falling.

Living in Colorado over the past 13 years has exposed me to a whole new culture of outdoor sports. A few years ago I tried one of these outdoor sports—I gave rock climbing a try. It was a dumb idea. As a former linebacker who has never been able to do a pull-up, I had no idea what I was thinking. Why did I believe my fingers and toes would be able to hold my weight as I climbed up a wall on pegs that protruded no more than 2 inches? Even though rock climbing didn't work for me, I have a lot of friends who love to go climbing. One of them told me what it meant to respect the mountain when you climb it. He said the fear of falling motivated him to ensure his equipment was working properly and his straps were as tight as they needed to be. This fear also caused him to hold on tight when he climbed. He didn't want to fall, and this fear made him more careful.

As I think about leadership in the church I see a lot of similarities to rock climbers. I am terrified of failing morally and failing as a leader. This fear has caused me to ensure my safety in different areas. Morally I have guards set up in my life that build a hedge of protection around me. For example, I never meet with a woman (besides my wife) in my office alone with the door closed. I avoid one-on-one appointments with women over any sort of meal.

And my wife has full access to my Facebook™, Twitter™, and e-mail accounts. What areas of your life do you need to "tighten" or learn more about so that you can guard yourself from falling? Healthy fear keeps me holding on to Christ, and his unconditional love gives me the confidence to continually return to him.

11 Don't let the effectiveness of other ministries intimidate you.

I need to confess something: I'm a very competitive person. A friend from Texas told me he was attending the Second Baptist Church in his town—and I thought about how I would struggle not going to the *First* Baptist Church! My competitive nature has helped me in many areas in life, but when it comes to ministry it has caused me a lot of unnecessary frustration.

Think about the first thing we typically ask another leader when we get in a conversation about our ministries. We want to know how many people attend or are involved. We do this because it is easy to count how many people are in the seats—and we use this as a gauge to evaluate our "effectiveness" as leaders. But I wonder if this is God's primary barometer for success in ministry?

your inner life

Other ministries out there may have more people attending than you do and they may be effective in ways that your ministry isn't, but this should not keep you from being faithful in doing what God has called you to do. You can benefit from studying the strategies and systems of other organizations, but don't allow the devil a foothold in your heart by tempting you to covet what other leaders have accomplished. Above all else, remember that we are all on the same team.

12 The best barometer for spiritual maturity is how we view the success of others.

In the previous thought we discussed avoiding comparisons against other individuals or ministries that may have more visible success than we do. These types of comparisons can lead to envy, and envy is a catalyst to unhealthy perspectives as a leader. One way to determine the spiritual maturity of leaders is how they react to the success—or shortcomings—of others. A spiritually mature leader can celebrate with another leader who is successful in ministry, but a spiritually immature leader will gain a sense of satisfaction when other leaders fall short. Can you celebrate with the other ministers in your community? Can you call them up when you hear of a great ministry event or outreach they organized and congratulate them on a job well done? Or do you allow bitterness to grow in your heart?

Your answer reveals your spiritual maturity as a leader. If you find yourself struggling in this area, consider connecting with another church leader or pastor in your community. Find someone who will encourage and support you—and someone you can encourage and support. Partner together, and look for ways to experience life together. This will help you celebrate the wins in other people's lives!

13 Before you can be a great leader, you must be a great follower.

People who have learned the skill of following can grow into strong leaders. Following is a skill learned out of obedience, trust, and humility. Our team members are trained to continually be on the lookout for potential volunteers and ministry leaders, and one of the main qualifications we look for is how people respond to leadership. The way someone responds to someone else's leadership usually indicates that individual's leadership capacity, and it can give you a picture of how this person will respond as a leader.

This principle is vividly displayed in the world of sports. Many talented athletes simply refuse to submit to the authority of a coach. They believe that their skills will take them where they want to go and that their talent supersedes the coaching staff's strategy and leadership. These individuals rarely reach their full potential as elite athletes because they haven't learned how to submit to the authority of another.

At every level of leadership within the church you are accountable to someone. How do you respond to that leadership? Are you a servant at heart and do you serve those that oversee you? Or do you feel that you have all of the answers and don't need their leadership? Let me also ask this: What kind of follower of Christ are you? How do you respond to God's leadership? The answers to these questions will most likely reveal some things about the way you lead others. Being a great follower will take you further in life. As you lead your ministry think of the kind of follower you are.

 ## Leaders can only multiply what— and who—they are.

Ministries often want their leaders to add followers, but identifying, equipping, and releasing leaders moves you from leading a ministry to facilitating a movement of God. To reach this stage of leadership, we must be intentional at multiplying leaders. We as leaders can only multiply what and who we are.

How is your walk with Jesus—is it an intimate relationship that is continually growing? Are you seeking ways to improve your leadership and communication skills? If you said "yes," then you are in great shape to pour into young leaders and develop them. Ministries take on the personalities and characteristics of their leaders. If you are a leader who studies the Bible and seeks God intently for understanding and wisdom, then those in your ministry will eventually emulate these characteristics in their spiritual lives. This particular principle is imperative when developing a leadership development strategy for your team. Look in the mirror and ask yourself if you are the kind of leader you want others to emulate.

A spiritually mature leader shows personal concern for other people.

When I read though Scripture, I often come across verses and principles that surprise me. It is interesting to see what God says is important in life because often times it doesn't line up with what I feel is important. Examining the role of leaders through the lens of Scripture will reveal God's true heart for what strong spiritual leaders are intended to be.

The book of Titus gives us God's standards as we identify elders to help facilitate God's work in ministry. Buried in this list of requirements is an interesting comment about

your inner life

leaders in the church needing to be hospitable (Titus 1:8). Why is hospitality so important? When I think of hospitality, I think of offering coffee and cookies to people who come to my house—but God isn't saying that church leaders need to be good at baking or brewing coffee! There must be some other principle here that God wants to communicate. People who are hospitable have a desire to comfort people, and they care deeply about how others are feeling and what they are experiencing. They understand the importance of helping people belong and connect. And they pass on these values to the others around them. Let's be leaders that never underestimate the principle of hospitality in our leadership and ministries.

16 Character is what you do when no one is looking.

What we do in public develops our reputation, but what we do when we are alone reveals our true character. We as ministry leaders are often concerned with our reputation because it's what others see, and we think our reputation directly shapes our effectiveness as leaders. This is faulty thinking. The things we do in the dark—in private—impact our effectiveness as a leader more than the things we do in the light—in public.

What we do in private undoubtedly and eventually will be exposed in our leadership. Leaders who compromise in private areas will typically compromise in the public areas. Let's be leaders who don't live for the accolades and approval of other people, but leaders who seek to please the God who sees us whether we are alone or in the public eye.

core traits and values

17   Pursue righteousness—being in right standing with others.

Among Christians, the word "righteousness" is tossed around when it comes to our relationship with God. This word can be defined as being in right standing with someone. We experience "right standing" with God through the work of Jesus on the Cross and through our faith in Jesus as our Savior. But our righteousness also needs to spill over into the relationships we have here in this world, especially for those of us who are leaders.

Here's a simple test to determine whether or not you are in right standing with someone: When someone calls you and the name pops up on your cell phone's caller ID but you don't answer the call because you know you wronged that person, you know that you aren't in right standing with that person. I encourage you to sustain your relationships, and if you wrong someone, go make things right as soon as possible. You will be in right standing with this person, and you will also increase your influence and impact as a leader.

Practice sincerity—do what is right with transparent, caring motives.

Few things are more comforting than someone who cares for others with a sincere heart. Unfortunately, many people in positions of leadership seem to care for others, but as you peel back the layers you discover ulterior motives. Leaders with sincere hearts do what is right with other people in mind and don't expect anything in return. People will gladly follow leaders who are transparent and caring, but if they feel that there is an agenda behind your concern for them, they will be cautious with their emotions and may struggle to trust you.

As leaders we are in the business of building trust with people and leading them toward a future that they may not see for themselves. Be a sincere leader and examine your motives for doing what you do. If you are not able to be transparent with your motives, then there is probably something wrong with them. Above all, genuinely care for the people you are entrusted to lead.

Be responsible—know what is expected of you and follow through with it.

Succeeding or failing with your responsibilities has the potential to make or break your reputation as a leader.

Taking responsibility as a leader is about following through with your promises. It's frustrating to have someone commit to something but not follow through with it. As a leader, develop the discipline to be diligent in finishing your projects and responsibilities. If you say you are going to call someone back, do it. Agreeing to attend a meeting but then blowing it off will discredit your reputation as a leader and will affect other people's trust in you. When it comes to responsibility, under-commit and over-deliver. Let's be leaders who follow through with the things we say we will do. We honor God and the people we lead if we're diligent in following through with commitments we make.

20 Instead of saying things that are important, be known as someone who's obedient.

Leaders want to say and do things that will impact people. As a leader in the church you undoubtedly want to communicate important spiritual truths that others will comprehend and live out through their lives. However, in our quest to say things that people will remember, we may forget that we are called to live obedient lives. The way you live will impact people more than what you say.

Don't fall into the trap of trying to be clever with words—simply walk with God and be obedient to what God asks you to do. As you pray and study the Bible, the Holy Spirit will give you spiritual insights that you can communicate. Don't let the desire to say meaningful things supersede your longing to walk with God and respond immediately to what he calls you to do. Remember, actions speak louder than words and in leadership actions echo over longer periods of time than words do.

21 Focusing on others will keep the attention from continually being focused on you.

Self-centered people direct every conversation to themselves and what they are doing. Self-centered leaders fail to focus their attention on others. You can't effectively influence and lead people if you are constantly directing attention to yourself. When you are in a conversation with someone, ask good questions. People like to talk about themselves, and as you ask questions you are accomplishing three things. First, you are directing the attention away from you and toward the other person. Second, you are allowing that person to open up and share with you. Third and probably most important, when people talk about themselves, they usually relax a bit. When you ask sincere questions, you give people permission to tell you about their lives, and if you have a sincere heart, then you are building trust. Leaders gain influence through trust.

22 Stewardship is the essence of leadership.

As you study the Scriptures you see that God owns everything and we are simply stewards. As leaders, we often make the mistake of only equating stewardship to material possessions. We forget the fact that our position as a leader is also a stewardship issue. God is the ultimate leader of our ministries, and one day we will have to give an account for the type of leaders we were. How are you investing your leadership, and how you are leading the ministry and people God has entrusted to you?

When leaders see their role through the lens of stewardship, they begin to seek God's direction in every decision. God ultimately leads the ministry that you lead, and he allows you to be a part of what he is doing. This is a great honor that should be taken seriously. Seek God's counsel as you lead his ministry. You will be held accountable one day for your decisions and actions as a leader. Seeking God will allow you to be an effective steward of the influence you have been given.

23 If no one is following you as a leader, you aren't leading.

I have always enjoyed reading John Maxwell's thoughts on leadership. I always chuckle when I think of him telling

core traits and values 23

leaders that if no one is following their leadership, then they are only taking a walk. This funny quote challenges us as leaders. Take a look at your leadership. Who is following you? An equally important question to ask is "Who is NOT following you?" and why aren't they? People will follow someone they believe in, but if a leader does not walk with integrity and lead with passion, then it is unlikely they will have others wanting to follow them anywhere.

The essence of humility is accepting your strengths and being honest about your weaknesses.

There are many ways to define "humility." The best definition I've heard is that humility means accepting your strengths and being honest about your weaknesses. The leaders who are a pleasure to work with are leaders who are honest about themselves. Having weaknesses does not mean you are a bad leader; having weaknesses means that you are human! There are no well-rounded leaders; humble leaders appreciate this and find ways to raise up people around them to compensate for their weaknesses.

Help the ministry you lead by discovering and developing your leadership gifts, and work within those gifts. Trying to be someone you aren't will hinder the growth of your ministry and potentially frustrate people around you. Discovering your leadership gifts will also allow you to be on the lookout for people who are gifted in areas you aren't so that you can release them in these responsibilities. You will ensure that your ministry will run more smoothly, and you will create opportunities for others to be a part of key areas of leadership within the ministry.

25 Healthy leaders view their role as raising others up rather than elevating themselves.

The Apostle Paul wrote a very direct and encouraging letter to the church in Ephesus. This letter discusses a lot of different topics. There are a couple of verses that have really challenged me as a pastor. Ephesians 4:11 says, *Now those are the gifts Christ gave to the church: the apostles, the prophets, the evangelists, and the pastors and teachers.* This is a pretty straightforward verse, but look at what comes right afterward, when Paul says WHY God has given these gifts: *to equip God's people to do his work and build up the church, the body of Christ.* The role of ministry leaders is not doing everything; our role as leaders in the church is to raise others up and watch them lead.

There is something fulfilling about being the go-to person. It feels good to be the person that everyone looks to for

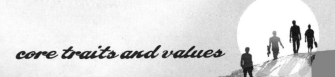

leadership and direction, but oftentimes we as leaders develop ministry structures with us at the center because we like the accolades and attention. Humble leaders accept who they are and what their role is. I want to encourage you to find people that you can raise up as leaders. Think about what would happen if you focused on the leaders that help lead the ministry. If you use energy to develop your leaders, then they will be better equipped to influence those within the ministry.

26 Good leaders are not balanced.

OK, I'm not talking about emotional or spiritual or relational instability here. I'm talking about one of the biggest myths we leaders tend to believe—we think we need to be well-balanced leaders. Don't try to balance your leadership; you will never be great in areas where you aren't gifted. The myth of the well-balanced leader can damage the effectiveness of the ministry you lead. When we try to be "well-balanced," we ignore the spiritual gifts we have been given to lead our ministries. For example, if you excel in communication but struggle with administration, then become excellent in communication and find someone to come alongside you to facilitate the administrative duties.

I'm not saying you should ignore areas of weakness. As a leader you will have to do administrative tasks whether you are gifted in administration or not, but don't spend your time trying to be excellent in administration if it's a weakness. Get others involved to help serve in areas you are not gifted in; this will ensure that you don't become a barrier to how effective your ministry can become.

27 Recognize that leadership is a marathon, not a sprint.

Over the years I have seen gifted, talented, young ministers burst on the scenes of high school and college campuses with incredible dreams and ideas of how God could use them to influence lives. Unfortunately many of these leaders faded away from ministry as quickly as they entered ministry positions. There is something to be said about the story of the Tortoise and the Hare—the focused Tortoise outlasted the speedy Hare—and how it relates to ministry leadership.

Take time to figure out your leadership style—and your ministry structure. I have witnessed the damaging effects of someone trying to change or launch ministry structures too quickly. Take your time when making changes or initiating ministry vision. You will avoid unnecessary pitfalls if you go slowly, and you will probably garner support from others who will want to come alongside you.

There is an old story of three young preachers who all came into ministry around the same time. Two of them were extremely talented and surpassed the third one in notoriety. But the two that burst onto the ministry scene quickly burned out. The third one, who didn't launch as quickly as the others, was Billy Graham—who went on to influence millions for God. Any strong organization takes a long time to build.

 ## Celebrate others' success.

You probably have your own definition for what it means to be a successful leader. But have you ever thought about your success being defined by the success of others around you? What if someone you lead ends up surpassing you as a leader? The ministry success Timothy enjoyed brought joy to the Apostle Paul's life, and we, too, should celebrate when those we minister to are successful in ministry.

It is natural for our flesh to develop feelings of envy when someone "surpasses" us in ministry, but if we are focused on the right priorities, then we will realize that we were used by God to develop a leader for the kingdom. Pray for the students and volunteers in your ministry. Pray that they will greatly surpass any accomplishment you have been able to achieve. We have the opportunity to train up the next generation of people who will make a difference for God.

This is a great and worthy task that should give us joy and fulfillment as we move forward in ministering to others.

I have a couple of students who came through our ministry and have gone on to ministry opportunities with other organizations. It blesses my heart to hear of the great things they are doing and to learn ministry practices from them. I encourage you to create a ministry that builds leaders— even if many of those leaders eventually serve other ministries. Being a kingdom-minded leader will allow you to celebrate the success of those you had the opportunity to influence.

 ## Ask the right questions.

Think about how you want to grow as a person and a leader. This will give you a head start in examining the current reality of where you stand as a leader. A good leader is able to examine the current reality within their personal life, leadership capacity, and ministry organization. Learn to ask the right questions. Think about where you want to go, and come up with questions that will help you get there. "Where am I going as a leader?" "Am I facilitating ministry settings that help us accomplish our goals?" "Do

core traits and values

we have goals for our ministry?" Questions like these are a great checkup on where you and your ministry stand.

Find a few leaders that you respect and ask them the same questions. Ask how they manage their time, what drives them in ministry, and what they have learned over their ministry careers. Questions like these will give you insight into their lives and can encourage you in your quest to grow as an effective leader.

30 | Make decisions based on truth, not emotion.

It's tough for leaders to refrain from making emotional decisions. As a leader, you will have to learn how to separate emotions from truth. I am a very emotional person, so if I'm not careful, I can allow my emotions to dictate how I live my life. I can be sky high one day and think that everything in life is going great, and the next day it will seem that everything is going wrong and I need to go find another career. The problem with this rollercoaster lifestyle is that it can all be based on whether or not I drink a Mountain Dew in the morning!

Emotions are a great gift from God, but we must learn to keep our emotions in check. The challenge is to keep our thoughts and our lives based upon truth. This is especially true for leaders. Our lives are tied closely to our ministries, so when something impacts our ministry, it often directly impacts our lives. Avoid making decisions when your emotions are high or raw. Take some time and think through your response, and weigh your options before you decide anything. This will help you make a wise decision rather than an emotional one.

31 Serving people is birthed out of a heart of love.

We rarely serve those that we don't love. Ministries that serve others typically have leaders with a heart for others. I recently had lunch with a student who wants to study international law at the local university. He is originally from Nigeria, and he said that he loves the people from his country so much that his life goal is to serve the under-represented. He wants to give his life away by serving people that don't have a voice in society.

Every established mission organization has been birthed out of a heart to make a difference in the lives of people with needs. If you love people the way the Bible calls us to love people, then you will develop a strong passion to serve them. Pray and ask God to reveal to you a certain group he would want you to influence. Do this consistently and you will watch your desire to serve this population grow.

32 An "inadequate" leader is a healthy leader.

I'll never forget one of the questions I was asked when I was being interviewed for my current pastoral position. A staff pastor asked me what made me nervous about being a pastor. Without even thinking I said that I feel so inadequate. At that point my work experience included lifeguarding, waiting tables, and coaching football. Some years later, I was talking to our lead pastor about that meeting, and he said that my response was one of the things they liked about me. Leaders who understand their inadequacy to lead leave room for the Lord to guide and direct their ministries. When I look for potential leaders, I am not always looking for the most talented or even the most driven leaders. I try to seek out people who are dependent on God. Being confident as a leader is not a bad thing, but we must avoid allowing our confidence to supersede our dependency on God.

33 Leaders view change as an avenue for growth and development.

The natural tendency for people is to resist change. People that resist change are not against growth; they simply enjoy the stability and comfort of doing things the way they've "always" been done. But leaders view change as an avenue for growth. Flexibility is key in leadership. People that resist when you see more effective ways of doing ministry may not necessarily be against you—they may just be uncertain of where you are trying to take them.

It is your job as a leader to reveal the benefits of the change you want to implement. If people don't see why a change needs to occur, they will not willingly adhere to the changes. Before you change anything, I would encourage you to consider these steps:

- Communicate the current reality
- Explain the challenges that the current system creates
- Share your vision for where you want to take the ministry
- Explain the benefits of the change

These steps may not alleviate everyone's concerns, but it will tell them that you have thought through the decision that you want the ministry to make. Don't be afraid of change—it may be the best way to grow the effectiveness of your ministry.

core traits and values

34   Leaders can only lead where they are willing to go themselves.

You will be a leader that others will want to follow if you demonstrate this principle. The strongest leaders are ones with a servant's heart. Someone with a servant's heart will never ask others to do something they themselves are not willing to do. Take the lead and be the example for others to follow. Words can only inspire people so much—your actions as a leader will communicate and inspire people more than words ever can.

Ministries always take on the personalities of their leaders. If you want your ministry to be a place where people study the Bible, then be diligent in your study of the Scriptures. Ministries with a focus on outreach must have a leader who is willing to step out and model what outreach looks like. Be the model for your ministry and don't ask people to do something that you aren't first willing to model.

35   Think outside the box.

The phrase "thinking outside the box" means thinking differently or looking at something from a fresh perspective. It takes creativity to think outside the box, and this is why creativity is a key trait of a good leader. The strongest leaders are not those who are the most talented or the ones with the highest level of education; they are the ones that are able to remove the brackets from current paradigms and think outside the box.

It's easy for leaders to continue doing things the way they've always been done. However, there may be creative solutions to doing things a little differently if we just take time to think outside the box. A great way to gain a fresh perspective is to talk with someone who has nothing to do with your ministry but who may be knowledgeable in the area you want to think differently about. We've struggled with balancing our ministry budget. None of our core leaders are financial experts, but there are plenty of men and women in our church who work with finances for a living. We have asked them to come alongside us, and through our conversations we have found new and fresh ways of balancing our budget. Sometimes thinking outside the box is a lot simpler than we think.

36 Genuine concern opens the door to hearing what you have to say.

As a leader, let others know how much you care for them before you ever try to tell them how much you know. If people don't trust you, they won't listen to what you have to say. Your theology degree and biblical knowledge mean nothing to those you serve in ministry if you don't take time to get to know them personally. When you first meet someone that you will potentially be discipling or bringing onto your leadership team, spend more time asking questions than talking. A great way to show someone that you care is to ask questions that will allow you to get to know more about this person. Learn about a person's history, childhood, spiritual journey, and dreams for the future. As you develop this bond with others, you will find that they will give you more and more opportunities to speak into their lives.

courage of a leader

37 Make fear your ally, not your enemy.

Some people have developed misconceptions over the years about leadership, courage, and fear. Think for a moment about "courage." How would you define that word? Many young leaders believe having courage means that you have no fear. I disagree. A courageous leader has developed the skill of moving forward in the midst of fear. As a leader, you can learn to view fear as an ally, not an enemy. Fear shows us how to be diligent and careful. Courage is a key element of leaders that make a difference.

I remember a time when I needed to make a tough decision for our ministry. We needed to change locations for our weekly gathering. At the time, we were meeting in a venue downtown, but we needed to move the gathering back to our church. I knew that the decision would be unpopular and that we would probably lose some key leaders in the process. I felt isolated, alone, and confused. I didn't want to make an unpopular call, but I knew it was the right one to make. As the leader I had to make the decision and navigate through the inevitable fallout. The fear of losing a few people because of a decision that you know is right for the overall ministry should never keep you from moving forward.

If we don't have a proper perspective on fear, it can paralyze us. Fear can be a great obstacle to moving a ministry forward—but only if we let it. We are called to be strong and courageous as followers of Christ and especially as ministry leaders. I'm not talking about leading blindly or recklessly. This can lead to foolishness; we must learn to think rightly about fear and courage before we can be effective leaders.

Confidence helps leaders move courageously.

How do we move from paralyzing fear toward courageous movement? The answer doesn't involve some complicated or theologically heavy principle. On the contrary, the answer is quite simple. Confidence is the vehicle that carries leaders from fear to courage, and confidence comes from knowing who you are. That's why it's so imperative that leaders know that their identity is based upon their standing in Christ and not what others say about them. Rest in the truth that you have been chosen to serve within the ministry you lead and that God has given you this opportunity to lead people. Rely on this God-honoring confidence to experience courage, even in the most difficult or fearful of times.

39 Communicate publicly what others are thinking privately.

There are always unsaid thoughts within any meeting environment, a phenomenon we have come to know as the "elephant in the room." As a leader you must be willing to say things that others may not be comfortable communicating. Your role as the leader of a ministry is not to ensure everyone's comfort; your role is to make sure that your ministry moves forward. This may require exposing circumstances and thoughts no one else wants to communicate. Be confident in the role God has given you and be open to talking freely about things that may be holding the ministry back, even if it leads to an uncomfortable conversation. This will improve your ministry effectiveness and will validate your authority as a leader.

40 Shine in an uncertain time.

One of the most important lessons I have learned as the central leader in a ministry is that uncertain times are unavoidable. Uncertainty used to scare me. I would fall into the trap of believing that if our ministry was facing an uncertain future, then I was a poor leader. But as I've

courage of a leader

traveled through the gantlet of ministry and life, I have discovered that uncertainty doesn't disqualify me as an effective leader. In fact, an uncertain future for our ministry gives me opportunities to rise up as a leader and move our organization forward. The best time for leadership to surface is when people don't know where to go. Situations like this are your time to shine as a leader. As you process and implement this principle in your leadership, I pray you are able to take advantage of the opportunities God gives you to lead and impact the world with the good news of Jesus.

41 Your best solution may not be the easiest one.

As you encounter difficulties and struggles in your ministry, commit to studying and growing as a leader. You will be called upon to make the final decision when troubles arise within your ministry. In some instances the same problem could be solved by two completely different solutions. Your job as a leader is to find the best possible solution that will help your ministry move forward. And most times the right decision won't be the easiest one for you or the other members of your team. As the leader you will have to clarify your reasoning and clearly explain what decision you are making and why. This may not sit well with everyone on your ministry team, but your goal is to discover the best solution, not the easiest one.

42 Practice courage during confrontation.

No matter who you are or what position you hold, as a leader you will need to have tough conversations with people. No one likes confrontation; if they do then there's probably something wrong with them! Confrontation isn't fun, but in leadership it is inevitable. I want you to consider a few points as you navigate through this necessary aspect of leadership:

Set up the meeting. If you never set up a time to talk about the conflict, you will never discuss it. Set up a time to meet with the person you are having the conflict with and let them know that you want to talk about what happened. Doing this will ensure that the conflict will be discussed and—you hope—resolved.

Stick to the facts. Conflict usually elicits emotions from the people involved. I encourage you to stick to the facts when discussing a conflict with someone. Our emotions can make clear situations cloudy, and when dealing with conflict, emotions can escalate a situation.

Let them share their perspective. If you allow someone to share their perspective before you "confront" them, you may find that the conflict stemmed from a misunderstanding. Two things potentially can happen when we give people the chance to share their perspective. First, you may start to think differently about the situation and find it

courage of a leader 41

resolved, and second, you gain trust from the other person for handling the situation appropriately.

Say the last 10 percent. Probably the most important thing in handling a confrontation well is having written documentation. Walk into the conversation with a list of what happened and what you want to discuss. When we walk into a confrontation without anything written down, we run the risk of forgetting details because of the tension or anxiety. Write down everything you want to discuss and make sure the meeting doesn't end until you have said everything you want to say. I've heard it said that the last 10 percent of a conversation is typically left out of confrontations, and it is usually this last 10 percent that cannot be omitted.

be a learner

43 Continued learning will lead to effective leading.

As leaders, we have access to more tools than at any previous time in history. The leaders of today's churches can read books, attend conferences, connect online, research topics, and listen to podcasts from influential church leaders from all around the world. Imagine what Oswald Chambers, A. W. Tozer, and Martin Luther might say today if they saw all the resources at our disposal! To become a great leader, learn and apply truths and principles about leadership. Spend time reading leadership books, and process what you are learning with other leaders who are in the same life stage as you. Listen to pastors, missionaries, and other ministers who have a ton of experience and want to share their stories. Be a student of leadership, because as you study AND apply leadership ideas, you will start to become a better leader. Remember—if you study leadership but don't apply the principles and truths, you're missing the point!

Read, read, read—but don't just read leadership books.

Yes, this is an ironic principle to include in a leadership book! Most leaders are drawn toward reading books written by prominent leaders and thinkers. But don't limit yourself as a reader. A long time ago, a mentor encouraged me to read three types of books—autobiographies, books on leadership, and fictional novels. These three types of books will allow you to process leadership principles and life principles, and they will ignite creative forces within you.

As I mentioned in the previous principle, books on leadership give you the opportunity to learn and apply ideas and practices that other leaders have discovered. Reading an autobiography will give you insight on someone else's walk with Jesus and will inspire you to live a life that glorifies God as well. You can learn some great lessons from people who lived lives of incredible faith. As you teach biblical truths, you will find that the stories of faithful men and women of God illustrate and clarify particular points. And fiction can keep you creative as you meet new characters and experience quality writing and storytelling. I encourage you to be a reader. I pray that you will gain insight from these different book genres and that you will grow as an authentic leader who serves God faithfully in ministry.

Learn from the experiences of your peers.

One of the most rewarding things you can do in your community is connect with other ministry leaders who are in the same role or life stage as you. In my town, I meet once a month with a group of ministry leaders to discuss the challenges and triumphs of ministry. This time together has proven to be very valuable. Some of us work at churches, some serve parachurch organizations, and some are teachers and educators. But we all are working toward the same goal. Spending time together gives us an opportunity to learn from one another.

This group has also facilitated connections among people in similar life stages. I spent about four years as a single guy in full-time vocational ministry. Being a single minister brings a whole lot of challenges, but having friends that were walking alongside me was comforting and valuable in my growth as a leader. I challenge you to get together with other leaders in your community who serve in the same or similar capacity you do. Learning from the experiences and situations of your peers will help you to develop into a healthy leader.

be a learner

46

Go spend time with other leaders.

Leadership is more caught than thought or taught. Find leaders who have been where you are, and ask them questions about their leadership and spiritual journeys. I spend a lot of time with pastors and former pastors who have been incredibly influential in my life as I walk through leadership and ministry. One of these pastors has been in ministry longer than I have been alive! It is easy for younger leaders to dismiss the insight of older leaders because our culture and the face of ministry have changed so much. However, the principles of Scripture and the underlying needs of people have not changed. I have found great insight in discussing ministry strategy with leaders who have led churches throughout the decades.

Connect with a pastor in your community who has pastored for more than 20 years and ask this person for some advice and wisdom for someone just starting out in ministry. Ask this pastor about preaching, discipleship, and strategies for balancing time and ministry. You will find the Holy Spirit starting to mold your leadership and develop you into a mature leader. I've discovered great openness from leaders within the church who have been ministering for 30, 40, and even 50 years—people who are eager to pour into the next generation. Take advantage of their willingness and their wisdom! Learning from their experiences will help you handle the challenges you may be facing.

If you let it, life will train you.

One of my favorite stories in Scriptures is the account of David and Goliath. You can find so many principles in this historical account. But the one thing that stands out to me has nothing to do with David throwing rocks at Goliath. I'm fascinated by the conversation David and Saul had when David volunteered to represent Israel in this showdown. Saul laughed at David for wanting to fight Goliath. The king told the shepherd that there was no way he could fight Goliath because the Philistine had been trained as a soldier and David had never been trained in the art of battle.

David replied confidently. He said that he was charged with keeping his father's sheep, and when a lion or a bear would come to attack the flock he fought them off. David was saying that life had trained him to fight this battle. For us as leaders there are great implications from this statement. If we are willing, life will also train us for the journey of leadership. Many of the things we experience today will encourage us and challenge and develop us as leaders for the future. We learned about social interaction and leadership from the sports teams and other groups we participated in as children, and discipline was developed as we studied for exams in school. If you let him, the Holy Spirit will use life situations to develop you into an effective leader.

be a learner

vision casting

48   Every idea leads to consequences.

It is easy to sit back and think of great ideas that will further the ministry you lead. However, we as leaders must account for the consequences our ideas may produce. Considering the impact of your ideas will increase your credibility when it comes to sharing those ideas with the people who will be affected. Here are a few things to consider before sharing ideas with your team:

- How does this fit into our ministry vision?

- Which leaders will be impacted with more work?

- How much will this cost?

- What other departments in our church or organization will be impacted by this?

These thoughts shouldn't keep you from doing what's in your heart, but they should prepare you to think about the work that will need to happen. A builder must count the cost before he starts building a house.

49   Take a step and trust God.

For most of us, vision casting in ministry is closely related to faith in God. Sometimes acting on faith requires us to do things and pursue things that don't make sense to other people. As a leader there are times when you must act on things that you don't see or understand. That's what it means to walk by faith and not by sight. Faith always fuels our understanding of God's vision for our ministries, and our action is a demonstration of the faith we have in the one we trust with our future. You are not responsible for acting on all the steps needed to fulfill a vision at once; you simply are responsible for responding in obedience to God with the first step. Then wait for him to show you the next step, and act on that. Wait for the next step, and then act on that. Keep repeating.

50   A dream will stay a dream without a plan of action.

Great leaders spend time dreaming and then coming up with a plan of action to make the dream a reality. It wouldn't do any good to sit and think about things but never act on them. Let me encourage you to take time to think of ways that your dream can become a reality. What resources can you utilize to fulfill your vision? How will you move forward and get other people on board? Try this idea: Start your planning by thinking about where you want to end up. Then work backward and come up with steps that will help you get to where you want to be. Working backward will help you think through the steps, processes, and systems needed to fulfill a vision.

Sharing goals with people will give you accountability to follow through.

There are a few guys in my life that I can share my thoughts with; they know that I'm a verbal processor and they don't expect me to follow through on every idea I share with them. However, these same guys know that when I write a goal down on paper, along with my plan of action, I'm asking for their help in achieving this goal. Sharing your goals with people you trust will give them an opportunity to help you follow through and will hold you accountable because you know that these friends will ask you about this particular goal and plan of action. Speaking things aloud to others can solidify your vision and direction in ministry and leadership. Be wise when choosing people to share your goals with; make sure they are people you can trust and people that you are comfortable allowing to speak into your life.

vision casting

52

Visionary ministries go after goals that are unattainable without God's intervention.

God-given visions are never easy. The best visions for our ministries and churches are often the most difficult ones to accomplish. If God is giving you a vision to influence, serve, and reach others, then it is probably a task you cannot accomplish without his help. It's easy for us to come up with visions and goals that we ourselves can attain. But God calls us to move in faith as leaders, and often moving forward in faith becomes difficult because we face obstacles that we cannot overcome without supernatural solutions. Don't be afraid of the unknown. If the Lord gives you a vision, then he will give you the resources and means necessary to follow through with what he wants to happen. Think big and trust God to show you the steps needed to achieve this God-given vision.

Imitating someone else's footprint will assure you that you won't leave a footprint yourself.

53

Here's a mistake many leaders make: examining what great spiritual leaders before them accomplished and then mimicking their methods in an attempt to achieve the same results. The problem with this is that we all have unique giftings and different callings as leaders. What worked for another leader won't necessarily work for you.

It is wise to study the stories of other leaders and the way God used them in ministry, but do this to gain inspiration and understanding of the principles they shared—not to figure out their methods and copy them. God desires to reach all of humanity, and he created unique leaders to reach different people. Figure out how God wired you and shaped you, and then move in obedience as a leader doing that. God has a unique calling and mission for each of us as leaders—let's figure out what it is, act in obedience, and watch God use us in mighty ways.

Discern the direction of your ministry.

Make no mistake about it. God has a call on your life, and people who are spiritual leaders and oversee a ministry are elevated to that level of responsibility and leadership by God. If God has placed you in leadership, then he has a plan on how you will bring him glory and influence others. It is your job as the leader to seek the Lord's will for your group and move people there. You are the one who is responsible for the direction of the ministry you lead. Yes, get advice and input from others, but make sure that you are taking responsibility in guiding the ministry in the God-given direction that he has revealed to you.

Lead by vision, not authority.

The best leaders lead by vision and not by position or authority. Anyone can lead people with force and title, but the best leaders inspire people to move together for a common goal. Managers utilize their position to ensure others do their part in an organization, but leaders move an individual or group forward toward a common goal. Find ways to reveal the vision that God has given you for your ministry, and encourage people to pursue it. The best way to move people forward in vision is to share with them the benefits of moving toward that vision and how your team effort will bring glory to God and impact others.

Don't forget to floss...your brain.

Daydreaming can be a blessing and a curse at the same time. Dreaming is a good thing, but if you stop at just a dream, what good is it? There are many ways that we can dream about making an impact within our churches, ministries, and communities. However, many of us never make it past the dreaming part. How can you move forward on a dream if you don't have the time, resources, or energy to see it through? There is nothing more frustrating than thinking of an idea that would impact teenagers or young adults and not being able to follow through with it.

You do not need to follow through with every idea; sometimes the best thing you can do is just sit on an idea.

And what do you do with these ideas? Sometime ago, a friend suggested I create a "Mental Floss" folder on my computer. This is where I "floss out my brain" and write down the ministry ideas bouncing around up there. This is a way I move forward with ideas without actively following through with them. The main advantage to writing ideas down is that you get the idea out of your mind and into written form. This means ideas won't be forgotten and can be reviewed at another time. I go back to my "Mental Floss" file a couple times a year to revisit my thoughts and see if our ministry is in a position to implement these ideas or strategies.

vision casting

building
a team

57 Raise up leaders who facilitate ministry when you are absent— and present.

As a ministry leader you need to raise up leaders who can facilitate the ministry you oversee when you can't be present. There are going to be times when you are sick, on vacation, or just need time away. It is OK for you to take time for yourself and have others oversee the ministry when you are not present. You can effectively "replace yourself" by spending time with your leaders, encouraging them, training them, and finding ways to release them. You can evaluate the effectiveness of leaders when they are able to develop others who effectively serve and minister when the core leader is not present.

However, it's even more powerful when a leader can be present—and have that same measure of confidence! Finding people to facilitate the ministry when you are not present makes you a good leader—developing others to facilitate ministry when you are there is the mark of an excellent leader. When you identify, train, equip, and release others to lead while you are present, you are obeying the biblical mandate from Ephesians 4:12, and this commitment will advance your ministry's purpose and impact. Imagine being able to walk into your gathering, talk to students, worship with them, sit down with them, and dig through Scripture while those you oversee are facilitating the ministry. Now that's shepherding the flock!

58 Surround yourself with people whose gifts and talents enhance yours.

As I talk to more and more ministry leaders, I am convinced that God has raised up strong leaders who are passionate about the Word, knowledgeable about culture, and excited about investing in students. However, I've also discovered that many ministry leaders are insecure about a lot of things—and insecurity manifests itself in unhealthy ways. I think you can pinpoint a leader's level of insecurity by the people who surround them. If leaders are truly secure in who God created them to be, they will surround themselves with team members who are more talented in certain areas.

Don't be afraid to surround yourself with people who are stronger than you are in certain areas. This doesn't make you a poor leader; on the contrary, it identifies you as a strong leader. Be comfortable with who God created you to be and where he has placed you as a leader. There is a reason that you are in this leadership position, so be confident in that. Your role is to facilitate what God is doing in the lives of people and shepherd them as their ministry leader. Nothing can take that away from you. Great leaders understand this and seek out others who are talented in their areas of weakness so the mission of God can be more effectively accomplished.

Leaders don't need all the answers; they just need to know where to get them.

Do you know how your ministry can best structure small groups? Are you unsure how to serve students from single-parent families? Are you struggling to find ways to connect with students that have questions about faith, or are you trying to figure out how to disciple the students who are already involved? These are hard but important questions. As you wrestle with the tough questions of your ministry, let me give you a word of encouragement: You aren't supposed to have all the answers.

I have agonized over and over about my role as a leader, and I've fallen into the trap of thinking that I needed to have all the answers to all the issues in our ministry. Guess what? It isn't possible for any of us! You don't and won't have all the answers, so stop worrying about figuring

building a team

everything out yourself. Find an expert in the field that you are wrestling with; seek that person out and ask for advice. Build a team of leaders with diverse skills and talents—and deep wisdom. We live in an age of digital information at our fingertips. A simple Google search can lead you to individuals and ministries that may be able to help you discover some good answers. And there are people in your church or community who can help you strategize. Great leaders don't have all the answers; they just know where to go to get the answers.

60 There is nothing like serving God with the people you love.

The other day I had lunch with a great friend of mine. We have been friends for a long time, and we've walked through many life situations with each other. We met our spouses around the same time, and we were in each other's weddings. We've also had the opportunity to serve God together in different ministry settings. As we were talking, I told him how passionate I was about working in a team environment—and more specifically, how much I enjoy teaming up with people that I genuinely love.

Working in a team environment is great, but serving Jesus and working with a team that you love is invaluable! I challenge you to find others that you love being around and people that you enjoy journeying through life with, and serve God with them. This will personally bless you, and I am certain that the ministry you lead will progress in the area of building strong community. Ministries mimic their leadership, and if the leaders are in strong relationships of faith, then others will grow into an effective faith community.

Clearly explain expectations to your team.

People who volunteer in the church want to do a great job. They choose to volunteer because they are passionate about certain population groups or issues or needs. They have time, energy, and expectations when it comes to satisfying that calling in their lives. But sometimes volunteers are not able to fulfill expectations set up by their leaders. As a leader there is nothing more frustrating than a volunteer not fulfilling your expectations. Where is the disconnect? Why are so many leaders frustrated that volunteers aren't fulfilling what they are supposed to—and why are so many volunteers frustrated because they can never seem to please the leader in charge?

I have seen this in my own ministry over the years, and one thing has helped us in bridging this gap more than anything: explaining our expectations. Writing out and agreeing to a ministry description will help you as a leader communicate your expectations, and it will give the volunteer a barometer to evaluate effectiveness. A ministry description doesn't have to be a super formal thing. Just write out what you as a leader would like to see, and let the volunteer look at it and speak into the description—the volunteer has a very valuable perspective as the person who is actually doing the ministry—and agree on it together. You will find this very helpful in effectively raising up and releasing others to do the work of the ministry.

Leading your team

62 | Not every situation needs your involvement.

Help your leaders grow by stepping back and allowing them to wrestle with tough decisions and situations. As leaders, we feel that we need to be involved in every decision, and yes, you should be involved in major decisions that are made within your ministry. However, there are probably many decisions that don't require your input.

Allow your team members to make decisions that will impact the groups and projects they oversee. This demonstrates that you trust them and value their opinion. It is imperative that you support your teammates, so if their decisions don't pan out, walk them through the process and discuss how they could have acted, led, or chosen differently. When you allow your team members to develop solutions to problems or systems to facilitate ministry, your team will develop and the ministry will grow further than it would if you were the only one making decisions.

When you make a mistake, admit it.

Leaders want to be perceived as people who say and do the right things. Nevertheless, you will fall short and you will disappoint people. I have seen leaders try to cover up their mistakes and errors, which often just makes the situation worse. If you mess up, simply come clean and let others know that you were wrong. Admitting our mistakes as leaders and asking people for forgiveness may not erase our wrongdoing, but it will develop trust and respect in the eyes of anyone we wronged. When we as leaders apologize for mistakes, people will be likely to forgive us and move on. We also show ourselves to be leaders worth following.

Every team needs managers and leaders.

There is a big difference between someone who manages a team and someone who leads people. Managers are able to get things accomplished and oversee key tasks and systems within a ministry. I have grown to appreciate the people within our ministry staff team who are gifted managers. Our ministry functions more effectively because of their gifts and talents. However, a team that is filled with managers is less likely to move forward and accomplish all that God calls them to do.

Leaders inspire others to go far beyond where they think they can go. If managers are critical to the functionality of a ministry, then leaders are vital to developing vision and goals. Healthy ministry teams have leaders and managers that understand each other's roles and are able to work cooperatively to accomplish the same task.

Are your spiritual gifts tilted more toward management or leadership? Take some time to think about this question, ask your friends and team members for their input, and pray for God's insights. Once you have a clearer answer, find at least one person for your team who can complement you with the other spiritual gifts. This way you will develop a well-balanced team and will ensure your ministry has the skills needed to be effective.

 ## Train leaders well.

For the first four years as a staff pastor, I found people cycling in and out of my leadership teams without any sort of consistency. I was frustrated, the leaders who came in and out were frustrated, and our ministry remained fairly stagnant. These people who stepped in and out of ministry leadership roles were dedicated, loyal, great men and women of God and were committed to watching people's lives change by the power of the Holy Spirit. The problem wasn't their commitment level; I was the problem. I did a poor job training them for their ministry roles.

If you spend time training your leaders well, you give them a head start in facilitating successful ministry opportunities. Training leaders isn't overly complicated. Think about what these leaders will be doing and walk with them through some material that will help them learn, grow, and develop. Look online and see what kind of materials are available to train ministry leaders, or call a church or ministry that is doing what you want your ministry to do and ask them how they train their leaders. Trained leaders develop effective ministries.

66 Release roles and responsibilities to those you trust.

If you don't allow others to lead in significant ways, then your ministry can never grow past your leadership capacity. This is a truth that must sink in if you want to develop a ministry that moves past you as an individual. You're probably doing things right now as a leader that someone else can do—and another person may even do these things better than you can!

As the leader, you are not responsible to do everything— you are just responsible for making sure things get done. Find people who are reliable, trustworthy, and full of the

Holy Spirit. Work with them, tell them the end result that you would like to see, and then release them to fulfill their ministry potential. You will release yourself from having to do everything, and you will develop leaders who may serve within the body of Christ for the rest of their lives.

67 Teams experience unity by reaching decisions together.

One comment I hear from leaders is that their teams don't seem to be on board with the decisions they make. If you want people to work FOR you, then tell them what you want them to do and oversee their progress. But if you want people to work WITH you, then include them in the decision-making process and the development stages of ministry vision and structure. If you want your team members to work alongside you in moving the ministry forward, then give them an opportunity to speak into the direction of the ministry. Don't just dictate what you want to see done.

When people realize they are a part of the decision-making process, they are more likely to invest their time, energy, and passion because they become personally invested in the vision. Even if the particular vision isn't what they proposed, you will see increased participation if you provide opportunity for their voices and thoughts to be heard, recognized, and valued. Don't dictate the direction of the ministry; work with a group of people and determine where the team feels God is moving you all.

68 Utilizing the strengths on your team is more important than finding the best talent.

Working within a team environment is vital to the health and progress of any leader. When you work with a team, you will be frustrated with your team members. You may even feel like replacing some of them! I remember one team meeting where my leaders just laid into me because of some things that I was doing as a leader. They were frustrated about their roles and did not agree with our direction as a ministry. Part of me wanted to "fire" them and find other people that would do what I wanted without all the hassle.

But over the years, these leaders became my greatest allies and our team's strongest supporters. These leaders will be the first to tell you that there are more talented people who can probably lead better than they can, but these leaders are totally indispensible. They have poured themselves into our ministry. When you walk through difficult times with people on your team, you develop a trust and a bond that can't be replaced by simply adding someone who is more talented.

People like this are much more valuable than talented leaders who have no personal interest in the work of the ministry you lead. For me, loyalty typically supersedes talent.

69. It is impossible to over-communicate with your team.

Communication is the No. 1 cause of frustration within work environments. Our team used to be horrible at communication. Some of us would know that we had a leadership meeting coming up, but other team members would have no idea until a couple days beforehand. Leadership teams in ministry can never over-communicate. There are many online tools available that help teams communicate effectively These tools can be a great benefit to your team's communication process, but nothing beats picking up a phone and talking to a person. Online communication and texting are great ways to give snippets of information, but make sure you are talking to your core leaders. Develop a system of communication on your team so that everyone is accounted for when something needs to be communicated to your team. Over-communication is far better than miscommunication or under-communication.

70 — Great leaders help team members identify their strengths, and then release them to minister.

Our churches are filled with faithful men and women who love God and believe in the mission of their congregations. These passions motivate people to get involved and step into ministry roles—even if it isn't the best fit with their talents and spiritual gifts. When people serve in roles that aren't a good fit, they typically burn out quickly and even start to resent their volunteer roles. As ministry leaders, we must help assimilate people into ministry roles that match their skills, talents, and spiritual gifts. Develop strong teams by being strategic as you release people into ministry.

One idea is to do personality profiles and spiritual gift inventories before you assimilate people in ministry. Many assessments are available to ministries; use a couple of these and give people the opportunity to serve in areas that are a good fit. This will improve ministry productivity and enhance the morale of the people serving alongside you.

71 — Delegate tasks, but don't forfeit your responsibility.

If you are the primary leader, you will always be the one who is ultimately responsible for decisions that are made within your ministry. You may delegate tasks to volunteers and other leaders, but you can never delegate the ultimate responsibility. One time some of our ministry volunteers used a church van to transport students to an outreach in our community. When the van was returned, it was littered with candy wrappers and trash. The next morning, our church's men's ministry wanted to use the van for an event. They had to clean up the mess left by our ministry.

Because I oversaw the student ministry, I was the person confronted by our church leadership. I was not present at the student outreach and I didn't drive the van, but I was ultimately responsible for my volunteers and their actions. As a leader you must be diligent in training and preparing your team for ministry, and you ultimately must take responsibility for the actions of your team members. When you accept responsibility for your team's actions, you develop a strong reputation among those you work with and become a great example of a servant leader.

Your team is an opportunity to influence people, not a means to get things done.

I learned a valuable lesson recently about leading a ministry: My team is not an extension of me to get things done. My team is a group of people that God has given me to lead and encourage. If you want your ministry to grow beyond your leadership capacity, then focus on pouring into your leaders and allow your leaders to minister to the people within your ministry.

As we read the Gospels, we see that Jesus focused his attention on developing his disciples—and then his disciples were charged with the commission of making disciples of all nations. As the leader you will see substantial growth in your ministry if you focus your attention on the people who lead alongside you. Effectively train, disciple, and release your leaders to go out and serve the masses. This will allow you to focus on a few influential people and develop a ministry that isn't based upon your role as a leader.

73 Encourage your team through regular phone calls.

Encouraging those you work with is essential in developing a healthy team environment. Talk with them and let them know you are thinking about them. If you communicate with your team members outside of ministry-related meetings, you will develop friendships and partnerships that go beyond serving together. A friend of mine suggested I encourage my team by calling them when I was on the road. I have written down the names of my key leaders on a 3x5 card that I keep in my car. When driving around town I pray for leaders on the list and then call them (using my hands-free device, of course). I let them know I was thinking about them and ask how they are doing personally. I then put a mark by their names and move down the list. If you go through your list a couple of times a month, you'll keep in touch with your team and you'll remember to pray for them and support them in their individual lives.

74 Unleash your team's potential instead of duplicating yourself.

It is normal for leaders to try to find people who will accomplish tasks they cannot complete. This is the conventional perspective on leadership. But if you want to develop a dynamic and thriving ministry, view leadership differently. Become a support for your leaders and your team rather than the authoritarian for your team. When you do this, you will start to grasp the picture of unleashing the potential of your team rather than duplicating yourself. God has surrounded you with uniquely gifted individuals who are passionate about ministering to other people. Develop the people around you and unleash the potential of your team members.

75 Sometimes "good enough" is good enough.

I tend to be a bit of a perfectionist. And I quickly found that my unrealistic standards were hindering my team members from doing what they were gifted to do. I was stifling their creativity by being controlling about the look of our fliers or the choices for songs in the worship service. Being around a control freak isn't fun, and being led by someone who micromanages is downright frustrating. I have started to look for instances where "good enough" is good enough. I realized that I was putting way too much time in things that didn't really deserve it. You'd be surprised how often good enough is good enough.

Your ministry will eventually run out of creative ideas if you have conditioned everyone to do things your way. When you release others to do things using their giftings and personality, you create an environment that has potential to flourish. As the leader of a ministry you are responsible to establish standards and direction for the ministry. To do this, lead like a compass. Give your team members general directions on where you want to go—but let them discover the details. When you do this, you will find that the work will get done, information will get communicated, and events will be planned. It may not be done the exact way you wanted, but remember: Sometimes good enough is good enough.

team meetings

76   **Meet regularly with your team.**

Some ministry leaders make the mistake of infrequently meeting with their teams. This may happen because of an overly strong sense of independence, failure to recognize the value of a strong team, or a deep dislike for meetings. I am not the biggest fan of meetings, but they can help create an effective team dynamic by providing a sense of camaraderie. Your team meetings can include elements like prayer time, ministry evaluation, upcoming event planning, and discussions of ideas and principles that will help your team members grow as leaders.

Jesus built a great team of people, and they went out and did life together. We have snapshots of insight regarding their ministry meetings. Mark 6:7-13 tells us of Jesus gathering his team, giving them instructions, then sending them out in pairs. Jesus even took advantage of long trips to have these meetings. On the way to Caesarea Philippi the "team" was asked about the identity of Jesus (Mark 8:27-30). Jesus also saw the opportunity to take his disciples along with him when he healed people. The healing of Lazarus must have created great conversation as they traveled the region. These were informal meetings, different from most "team meetings" these days. But the overriding principle is to regularly and consistently bring your team members together.

Quality of meetings is more valuable than quantity of meetings.

While meetings are important for building your team, avoid the trap of having meetings for the sake of having meetings. Time is a valuable resource for you and your team members, and you will go a long way in establishing a dynamic team if you are sensitive to this. Quality is more valuable than quantity when it comes to meetings.

The frequency and type of meetings you have with team members will be directly related to their role. I meet with some leaders weekly because these people are more involved and have assumed a lot more responsibility. I connect with other leaders on our team monthly. They have significant roles, but the ministries they lead pretty much run themselves, so our monthly connections are for encouragement and planning. Sometimes I have one-on-one meetings, and sometimes I meet with a large group of leaders. Be sure to put thought into the meetings you have with your ministry leaders and volunteers. You and your team will benefit greatly from quality meetings.

78 Be fully present in meetings.

As a leader, you're responsible for organizing and guiding meetings—but you're also probably required to participate in meetings directed by your supervisor or other leaders in your ministry or organization. Model the kind of behavior you want to see from the people in YOUR meetings by participating and engaging.

Technology gives us the opportunity to stay in touch with people whenever and wherever we want. This can be a good thing, but we should refrain from being "connected" when we are in meetings. I have been in a lot of one-on-one meetings with students and leaders who will take out their phones to respond to a text message while I am talking with them. I have also been in team meeting environments where people have their laptops open and check e-mail while others are talking and interacting.

If you respond to a text message or check your e-mail during a meeting, you are communicating to others that they are not important to you; the person you are responding to is your focus. I have tried to make a habit of not taking my phone into meetings or ministry settings. I encourage you to take a pad of paper to meetings for notes. You may be taking notes on your phone or laptop, but it has the potential to communicate that the people

team meetings

you are meeting with are not important enough to capture your attention. And remember: The way you behave in other meetings will become the way your team members behave in the meetings you lead!

79 If you don't come up with the meeting agenda, someone else will.

Having goals in life and pursuing them will help you live with purpose. Having an agenda for your team meetings will help your organization move toward effectiveness and demonstrate that you're meeting for a reason and purpose. Establishing an agenda will let everyone know what you want to discuss and where the meeting is going. People want to belong to something that is moving forward. There isn't really anything inspiring about a group of your volunteers sitting around a room staring at each other, wondering what to say next. Encourage open conversation, of course, but as the leader, guide the direction of your team's discussions. Consider allowing team members to speak into the agenda before you meet. Give them a deadline and tell them that you need agenda items two or three days before the meeting takes place. You will see a renewed sense of involvement and passion if your meetings have purpose.

Being prepared for a meeting will communicate authority.

Have you ever participated in a meeting with someone who wasn't prepared at all—even though this person was leading the meeting? I tend to lose interest when I am a part of a meeting that has an unprepared facilitator. If you are facilitating a meeting, be prepared for the meeting before it starts. This principle goes beyond setting a meeting agenda. Make sure all handouts are copied and information is researched before you step into a meeting that you are leading. This will communicate your trustworthiness as a leader. Spend at least 20 minutes before each meeting you lead reviewing the agenda, notes, and any handouts you will cover. I have this time blocked off in my calendar so that I am sure to have time to prepare for meetings I lead.

Create unusual but effective team meetings.

The worst thing about routine meetings is that they become, well, routine! Finding ways to change up the pace and place of your meetings will stir up creative juices and help your team build strong relationships. Here is an example of how I facilitate this with my team.

After weeks of intense planning for our upcoming ministry semester, I sensed that my team was burning out a bit. I knew that we needed a change of pace, so I vowed to keep the next month of meetings fun and exciting. I told the team to gather at our regular time and bring everything they needed for our meeting—but the location would be a surprise. For four weeks, we would load up into a church van and our team had no idea where our meeting was being held until we reached our destination.

We didn't do anything special. One week we went to Starbucks and another week we went to Chipotle. I had also scheduled some time for us to get to know each other by going to a local ropes course.

Find ways to change up your regular meeting routine. Meet at someone's house, or just go to a park and have some fun together. Our team paintball adventure still elicits laughs and memories that have helped bond our ministry team.

 Some of the best meetings have nothing to do with ministry.

As we examine the Gospels, we observe Jesus investing in his disciples by doing life with them. We read stories of this team traveling from town to town, spending time together, and simply experiencing life with each other. Ministry is about building relationships with people and discipling them. As you build your team of leaders, never underestimate the value of simply being with your team members. Spending time away from ministry settings and doing life with them can be just as effective in the discipleship and team-building process as sitting down and discussing Scripture. These experiences allow the people on your team to see you live out your faith—and this will speak louder than any sermon you could ever preach. Invite others to join you when you work out, run errands around town, or work on a project at your house. Eat meals with your leaders after services and events. My wife and I have found that inviting people over to our house provides great opportunities to speak into the lives of those we serve. We build trust when we include them in our lives, and we learn a lot about life from them as well.

team meetings

time management

83 | Focus your schedule around your life roles.

We all have 168 hours in a week, and the most productive people have learned how to steward that time effectively. One way to effectively use your time is to identify the roles you have in life and designate certain times to these roles. Have you ever sat down and written out the different roles you have? I challenge you to work through this exercise because it will help you plan your time and become more effective in leading a ministry. After you identify your roles, spend some time planning out how much time you want to spend in each role.

For example, let's say you are a husband, father, youth worker, and volunteer at the local fire department. Your challenge is to determine how much time to spend in each role. You can do this for each week or for a month at a time. I sit down weekly and plan out when I check my e-mails, return my phone calls, and schedule meetings with people. I have learned to run my calendar and not allow my calendar to run me. You can do this, too. Establishing this discipline will ensure that you spend adequate time accomplishing the tasks before you. When you budget your time effectively on these major life roles, you will discover plenty of time in a week to do everything that needs to be accomplished.

When you are always available, you won't be effective when you need to be available.

Ministry is tiring. You are responsible for overseeing settings and ministries where people encounter Jesus, but you also need to spend time studying for teachings, preparing for meetings, and planning for future events and programs. Ministry workers face incredibly tiresome demands. And many of us also face overwhelming expectations from others. Trying to meet everyone's expectations can drain us physically, emotionally, and spiritually.

I want to give you permission to not always being available for others. When you are continually accessible for meetings, phone calls, or counseling appointments, you rob yourself of time to recuperate, reflect, and rejuvenate. Being available everywhere and in all situations will ensure that you won't be effective anywhere!

Even Jesus needed to escape the crowds so he could spend time with his Father. Don't feel bad if you need to get away—even if there are people in need. God will take care of them, and what people need is a healthy minister who is well rested and in tune with the Holy Spirit. You cannot be this person for others if you are continually available and spread thin.

When it comes to big events, plan ahead.

Planning ahead will help your team be as prepared as possible when getting ready for big events. Learning and applying this principle will help you lead effectively and help your events avoid pitfalls. When you spend time thinking through potential snags on the front end, you'll spend a lot less time solving problems while you are trying to minister, serve, and connect. For example, if you are planning a retreat, spend time with your team thinking about potential problems that may arise and determine a course of action ahead of time. Or if you are planning an outdoor event, spend time thinking about an appropriate plan of action if the weather doesn't cooperate. Have options and know the best ways to respond. And if you're organizing an event you've done before, consider the problems from previous years and discuss ways to prevent them. You will find that planning is a great ally in creating events.

86 The more you prepare, the less you will repair.

Those of us who are involved in leading ministries want to see people's lives impacted by Christ. However, when we as leaders are spending time "repairing" a ministry, we are prevented from spending time ministering to people. The best way to limit how much you need to repair your ministry is to spend more time preparing—especially if you're ready to start a new ministry.

For example, if you are about to launch small groups within your ministry, think through as many potential scenarios as possible before you start. If you and your team find yourselves ill equipped to support the leaders or groups, consider delaying your launch until you're ready. It's usually better to postpone the launch of a particular ministry than to start before you're ready. Be patient and don't rush ministry opportunities because you feel the pressure to start something. Think through the ministry before you start it. Ask your team members if they see any potential pitfalls or problems that need to be addressed before the ministry launches. This will ensure that you and your team establishing strong and sustainable ministries.

Don't be busy—be effective.

Being busy and being effective are not the same thing. Many of us are great at being busy, but it takes intentionality to be effective. Great leaders position themselves and their lives to achieve the greatest amount of effectiveness. Just being in your office doesn't mean that you are getting things done. I have found that if I give myself a time limit in getting a project done, I am much more efficient with my time and energy. Being an effective leader means being an intentional leader. Be a leader who is intentional with your time and not simply a busy person!

Avoid "time wasters" that make us seem efficient but really just cause us to be busy. If we don't get a handle on managing our time, we will find ourselves falling into the trap of these time wasters. E-mail, Facebook™, and phone calls can waste our time—even though they're all valuable and essential tools in ministry. Let's take e-mail, for example. We in ministry get a ton of e-mail. I quickly had to learn that I couldn't immediately respond to every e-mail that entered my inbox. So, I carve out four blocks of time for responding to e-mails: in the morning when I get to the office, right before lunch, in the middle of the afternoon, and right before I leave the office for the day.

Facebook™ and other social networking sites have become huge tools in reaching people and building relationships— but they also can become time wasters. I spend about 25 percent of my time each day writing my blog, connecting with people, and sending ministry updates—but it's intentional time, and I have had to carve out time to do this. My prayer is that you would be an effective leader who is able to run your calendar and work efficiently as together we spread the message of Jesus.

the ministry you lead

88   Ministry grows as leadership grows.

An effective ministry grows through the commitment and involvement of effective leaders. Be cautious about launching new opportunities within your ministry before you have the necessary leadership. It's unfortunate to see the birth of ministries that later died because of inadequate leadership and support. The more time you spend developing a specific leader before you release them to lead, the better equipped that leader will be to oversee and sustain a viable ministry group. Let's develop ministry opportunities that have adequate leadership to support them; this will help ensure the strength of ministries we oversee.

89 Trustworthy words and deeds build trustworthy leaders.

In Matthew 5, Jesus says we should be trustworthy in our speech. "Let your yes be yes and your no be no" is a great reminder for us as leaders. There are obvious repercussions when we go back on our word. Are your actions and your words consistent?

We as leaders are called to care for and shepherd the people that God has entrusted to us. We are not effectively caring for people when we don't follow through with them. People are counting on us, so we must maintain this trust. If you say you will be at a meeting, be there. If you promise someone a phone call, then call.

Obviously, in ministry we will never be able to fulfill every expectation that every person places on us. Following through doesn't mean we do everything that others demand of us—it means that we acknowledge the people who trust us. When someone e-mails you, write back within 24 hours (unless you are on vacation or your day off), even if it's simply an e-mail saying you cannot respond in detail immediately but will do so as soon as you can. Nothing breeds care for others like following through, keeping your word, and communicating with them.

90 You can still have intimacy in large groups.

Many people fall into the trap of believing that the number of people present determines the intimacy of a particular ministry setting—particularly the idea that you can't have intimacy if you have lots of people. But intimacy isn't based upon the number of people in attendance; intimacy is based upon the honesty and transparency expressed by those who are present. As a leader you are challenged with the role of developing ministry opportunities where people can freely share their thoughts, emotions, and lives with one another. When you are able to do this you will see an intimate ministry develop.

91 Your community's needs create opportunities to serve and minister.

Many young leaders try to take a program that is working in one city and establish it in their local neighborhoods. After all, there are ministries all over the world that are doing amazing things within their own communities; can't we just duplicate and replicate these ideas in our own backyards? Sometimes we can. But many times, it won't work because a ministry effort that works well within one context may not work well in another. Consider this: Your greatest ministry opportunities in the next 12 months may not be things that you have planned on—they may be moments when your church can meet an unexpected or unmet need within your local community.

Evaluate your city. What are the needs? What people group needs attention? How can your ministry make a difference? Gather some of your leaders and go ask city officials, school principals, or social workers what you and your organization can do to serve the community. After you get some answers, go back and discuss the opportunities with your team. Search for ways that you can help meet these and other needs. Who knows what God will do as you serve others!

A strong foundation is key in taking advantage of opportunities in your community.

Ministries need a strong structure to take advantage of serving opportunities that arise within their community. As the leader it is your job to ensure that your ministry develops effective structures, systems, processes, and procedures; this is particularly essential as you reach your community and your ministry grows. The strongest elements that develop a solid foundation for a ministry are relationships and leadership. Developing leaders and providing ways for people to connect with one another will create a strong structure for your ministry. When these foundations are set, then you and your ministry will be positioned to make an eternal impact within your community.

93 Get people together—and send them out.

The old adage "strength in numbers" rings true in ministry. Think about what would happen if you got a handful of trained leaders together from your ministry and commissioned them to go out and find ways to spread the good news of Jesus, either in word or deed. When people serve alongside at least one other person, their work is multiplied. Unite a couple of passionate Christians together, and their potential is limitless. Be kingdom-minded and send people out together into the community to spread the good news of Jesus.

94 Believe in people.

One of the greatest statements you can make is how much you believe in a person. I challenge you to not just say it, though; I challenge you to really believe in the people you oversee and lead. God has gifted every Christian with spiritual gifts, and everyone has the capacity to impact the world for Christ. We often focus on those within our ministries who show the most obvious potential. But if we believe what the Bible says about the kingdom and God's love for all his children, then we would see every individual as a crucial part of the spreading of God's kingdom.

Develop avenues for people to be involved within the ministry of God. Let everyone within your ministry see their role in the mission of God, and encourage them as you release them to serve God. Your words and your validation of their role in the kingdom will do more than you know in the lives of those you shepherd.

Create avenues for people to speak into the ministry.

One of the best ways to move your ministry forward is to create avenues for people to speak into the direction of the ministry. To do this effectively, be strategic in processing a wide range of opinions. Here are a few tips on getting others to speak into the direction of the ministry:

- Don't give people the expectation that every suggestion will become a reality.

- Be selective in who you allow to provide input into the direction of the ministry. Leaders and committed members of the ministry are great people to provide insight.

- Before a meeting, think about some of the ideas people might suggest, and consider preparing possible responses or suggestions so that people have an idea of where you see things going.

One thing I have learned in leadership is that I can get input from others and release my team to go out and do the things that God has placed on their hearts, but if something goes wrong I cannot put the blame on them. At the end of the day my supervisor will come to me if something goes awry.

96 You can't always evaluate ministry success by the current reality.

As I have progressed in ministry leadership, I have found that evaluating the effectiveness of a ministry can be challenging. Oftentimes the current reality is a poor way of determining success. Ministry is about lives being impacted with the message of Jesus, and this process involves intentionality and time.

Right now, you may not feel like you're making any sort of difference in people's lives. Be patient. I've received phone calls from former students saying that Jesus became real to them years after they spent time in our ministry. They've thanked our team and me for the prayers and ways we

the ministry you lead

encouraged them. Remember: As a leader, you have the opportunity to view ministry from an eternal perspective.

97 Clarity will encourage and facilitate movement.

When things are unclear, people are less likely to move forward. However, when vision is presented plainly, people are quicker to respond. To ensure clarity for a ministry, identify clear and concise steps that will get your ministry to a desired destination. As a leader one of your roles is to get people to move from inaction to action. Those in your ministry may not always foresee the future for the ministry as you see it; communicating this vision is part of your job as a leader. Think about where you want people to be and where you want the ministry to go, and develop a clear strategy to communicate this.

98 Create compelling ministry opportunities.

We changed the trajectory of our ministry by developing compelling leadership opportunities for people. We already had leadership roles, but often these opportunities were developed to serve us as the staff because there was more work than we could handle. During one of our many structure evaluations we realized that we did not allow people to join in the work of the ministry in compelling ways. In effect, we were hoarding the work of the ministry and delegating the things we didn't want to do. This limited the involvement and interest of potential leaders within our ministry. We quickly developed ways in which people could join the staff in ministering in significant roles. Who knows what talent could be hiding within your ministry. If you don't provide ways for people to get involved, you will never see these hidden talents unleashed.

One specific example is the training up of our small group leaders. I had a structured leadership development plan for training our small group leaders. Eventually we found a couple of people to help oversee our small groups. One guy within our ministry really wanted the opportunity to teach and train leaders. We met for a few weeks and planned out the teaching topics for small groups and the training process for small group leaders. I essentially handed the small group ministry over to him—after weeks of discussion and planning. He led our small group teaching for a semester, and he changed the trajectory of our small group ministry by bringing in fresh ideas and energy to the small group leaders and the small group ministry. The leaders were trained better than I ever could have trained them because he had the time, passion, and energy to build relationships with the leaders— and this translated to more effective small groups for our ministry.

99 Partner with the greater body of Christ in your community.

Are you interested in building God's kingdom in your city—or building your kingdom? One way to gauge if you are kingdom-minded is how you respond to the idea of partnering with other ministries in your community. No matter where you live, your community is way too big and diverse for you and your ministry to reach every person with the good news of Jesus. Partnering with other ministry leaders is crucial in reaching people who need to experience God's love, grace, forgiveness, and abundant life. As you partner with other ministries, you will find that they are able to reach people that you can't—and you are able to reach people they can't. Impacting and reaching a city for Jesus is a team effort. I encourage you to be the catalyst that brings leaders together to strategically develop ways that your partnership can glorify God and reach your community.

communicating
and connecting

100   Be the person God made you to be.

The incredible team at Apple developed one tool helping shape the way ministries communicate: iTunes. This program has reshaped the way we listen to music, and in the church world it has helped us reach people that we never thought possible. Podcasts allow us to broadcast sermons and teachings to anyone in the world. Podcasting also gives us, as leaders, the opportunity to listen to many talented preachers and Bible teachers. This can be a great thing, but it also may hinder the development of many leaders.

This past year, I stopped listening to podcasts. (Yes, it felt like heresy at first—a church leader avoiding podcasts!) For a while, I had listened to a different Bible teacher each day. On Mondays I would listen to Andy Stanley, on Tuesdays it was Erwin McManus, Wednesday brought me to Chuck Swindoll—I love the classics!—and so on. As I prepared my messages I found myself emulating these different speakers' teaching styles rather than trying to find out how God had uniquely shaped me to teach. Obviously there is nothing wrong with listening to other Bible teachers; it can be a great habit to develop, but not at the expense of exploring your personal teaching "style." God created you to be a leader with a unique style of speaking and leading. Take some time exploring who you are as a leader and how you are uniquely shaped. During this process, you may find yourself experimenting a bit, but that's OK. I encourage you to be patient as you discover who you are. Wishing you were someone else is a waste of who God has created you to be.

Spending time with people on their turf can help lower the walls around their hearts.

Every person that walks through the doors of your ministry wants to connect emotionally with others. We were created with a need and a desire for healthy relationships. As spiritual leaders we are called to speak truth into people's lives and watch the Spirit of God change their hearts. But because of the hardships and circumstances of life, many people have built walls around their hearts that prevent love and truth from penetrating. What if someone is so calloused to life that the walls around their heart won't allow us to communicate truth?

I've found that people will often lower their defenses when they're doing things that they enjoy—or when they're just smiling and laughing. This is where you as a leader have the opportunity to creatively connect with people. Spend time with them, get to know more about them, and discover why they've built these defenses. If you commit to getting to know others on "their turf," you will find them opening up to you and listening to you in ways they didn't before. That might include spending time at the gym working out or playing basketball. It could mean visiting someone's workplace or school campus. Find and create settings where people will be more relaxed and more open to honest conversation and connection.

102 Discover ways to communicate life principles in all situations.

One of the biggest objections I hear about the Bible is its seeming irrelevance to this culture. People remain convinced that the Bible is outdated because it was written thousands of years ago in other languages in another part of the world. While it's true we must process the Bible with an awareness of its original culture and context, the principles we find in Scripture remain timeless and have the potential to impact our lives today. As leaders we can help people discover the truths that Jesus spoke about or Paul wrote about. Helping them see these principles lived out in their lives is a far better teaching technique than 10 sermons preached.

communicating and connecting

Be sensitive to the prompting of the Holy Spirit as you interact with people and help them see how God's truths are being revealed to them. The only way to effectively do this is to spend time with people. The longer we've been Christians, the easier it is to forget what it's like to explore the claims of Christianity. Spending time with people will expose you to their life situations and give you opportunity to share the principles of the Bible with them.

103 Focus on who is in attendance, not who isn't.

Have you ever prepared for a service or event and in the end been disappointed by the attendance? It can be demoralizing to do everything you can to create a great environment but not have the numbers you wanted. Unfortunately, as leaders we often focus on who is not there, instead of who is in attendance. The worst thing we can say in this situation goes something like, "Well, where is everyone?" When we say this, we inadvertently devalue everyone who showed up. When it's obvious we are disappointed in turnout, we are essentially telling the people who attended that they don't matter. On nights with lower attendance, we make it a point to thank the people who came and let them know how much we appreciate their participation. What would happen if every person that walked through the doors of our ministries felt significant and valued?

We would be doing what spiritual leaders are called to do: Show people how important they are in the kingdom of God.

Focus on the people you are talking to rather than directing attention to how smart you are.

A friend told me a story of one of his first preaching opportunities when he was in seminary. He was invited to speak to his old youth group, and the pastor who invited him had been his youth pastor for many years. My friend was excited to share about some of the things he was learning in seminary. When the service was over, my friend felt really good about what he said and the way he communicated. But after all the students had left, my friend's former youth pastor came up to him and seemed pretty frustrated. He asked my friend, "Do you even care for kids or do you just want people to see how smart you are?" My friend used a lot of theological terms and concepts that were way above the heads of these students. It can be valuable to communicate original Greek terms and theological concepts when we preach, but we must be sure these illustrations point people toward Jesus and not our own intellect.

Build sermons around one main thought that people can apply.

I recently sat through a sermon at another church and left the service confused about what the pastor wanted to communicate. There were 10 fill-ins on my note sheet, and we jumped from topic to topic. Those of us who were trying to follow along ended up closing our Bibles because we couldn't keep up. The reality is that people will not remember all of our points we communicate—especially if we communicate to teenagers or young adults. The best advice I got about preaching was focusing on what you want people to think, feel, and understand when they walk away from your teaching—in other words, one main idea that is relevant to your audience.

In today's church culture, our sermons often have an intro, Scripture thoughts and explanation, and about five minutes of application at the end. But if you study the teachings of Jesus and the letters of Paul, you see how spiritual truths were revealed and how different stories and thoughts created opportunities for life application. Let's be communicators who simplify our messages and show people what it means to pursue lives that apply the truths of Scripture.

106 Teach values, not methods.

One pastor who has drastically impacted my life, ministry, and leadership tells of his childhood and how for him Christianity seemed to be a list of rules that he had to follow rather than a lifestyle to live. Think back to the things that you do in your daily walk. For many people we minister to, spiritual disciplines are requirements or expectations for people following Jesus, rather than values that express our gratitude to God for his goodness.

When we as leaders teach the truths and principles of Jesus, we are inviting people into a life of expressing worship to God, not a checklist of things they need to accomplish to show God how much they love him. Jesus didn't share methods of living a godly life. Rather, he taught people the values of the Father, which gave people freedom to express their love to God in unique ways. Let's be leaders who refrain from telling people how to live. Instead, let's be leaders who point people toward Jesus and allow the Holy Spirit to direct their lives.

communicating and connecting

107 When confronting someone, listen to the person's perspective before you say anything.

No one likes confrontation, but it's an inevitable part of leadership. One leader who has influenced me is so great at confrontation. One time I walked out of his office after I needed to be reprimanded—and I had a smile on my face, and I was excited that I was on a journey of leadership and this was just one step in that journey. How did he do that? I have often wondered how he got me to feel good about that difficult confrontation!

I've been part of many different confrontations—I was in the middle of things or had the opportunity to mediate—and one principle has always stood out to me. When you give people the chance to share their perspective, you can usually see why they made certain decisions, and confrontations are typically easier to handle. One thing that helps people share their perspective is to ask them about the situation before you say anything. Start the conversation with a phrase like "Tell me about _____." This will give people the freedom to share their perspective and give you insight into their thought process. You will usually find that people weren't attempting to make others mad or create problems, so there was probably a breakdown somewhere along the way. Being able to talk about that will help alleviate tension, and maybe when you verbalize that breakdown, people will leave your office smiling about the confrontation.

Do right, don't be right.

It's probably already happened to you. If you are in any kind of leadership position, someone has done something to really get your blood pressure skyrocketing. Let's face it: People are people, and as long as we are in ministry we will have to deal with them. The problem with people, is that they mess up. Of course, we as leaders are people too—and we also have the tendency to make a mistake or two! What we do when someone makes a mistake says a lot about who we are and how we can grow as leaders. Our natural tendency is to prove that we are right and make a point of clarifying our position. However, as a leader you may need to set your pride aside and simply do right instead of being right. We have the ability to lead by doing right instead of justifying ourselves in these tough circumstances.

Use social networking effectively.

The phenomenon of social networking has taken our culture by storm. MySpace™, Twitter™, Facebook™, YouTube™, Blogger™, and WordPress™ are just a few websites and tools that have revolutionized the way we communicate with each other. Our students are sharing pictures, inviting one another to events, and uploading videos on these sites frequently each day. These websites have the ability to enhance the way we disciple, interact with, and connect with people in our ministries. Many leaders who've begun using Facebook™ or Twitter™ or want to start a blog have the same question: "What do I say?" Here are three ways for leaders to build consistency and credibility on social networking sites:

- **Introduce yourself.** Let people know who you are. Social networking gives us the opportunity to tell people about us. Introduce yourself, your family (if you're comfortable with that), and your hobbies. Sharing insights like places you grew up or went to school can help build bridges to people in your ministry.

- **Share your life.** Sharing funny things you are thinking or favorite quotes will give people a chance to see you apart from your ministry role. Update people on places you like to eat or where you spend your time away from ministry. This will give people an opportunity to understand who you really are.

- **Pastor people.** Using social networking to pastor people is a growing trend among church leaders. Lead your congregation from the comfort of your couch. Consider doing a blog series through a book of the Bible, or simply tweet a Bible verse daily. If you are consistent with this, you will find that you will develop a trust with people that goes beyond them showing up at your weekly gathering.

110 Social networking can benefit your ministry.

About 25 percent of my ministry time is spent on social networking sites. I am a daily blogger, and I update my Twitter™/Facebook™ status a couple times a day. Our ministry uploads announcement videos on YouTube™ weekly, and social sites like Facebook™ and Twitter™ have allowed us to gather impromptu BBQs and game nights for people within our ministry. I have seen tweets and status updates enhance the discipleship process by reintegrating thoughts I emphasized in a previous teaching. Here are a few thoughts on how you can effectively use social networking in ministry:

- **Introduce upcoming sermon topics.** Let people know what you are studying, and prepare them for the upcoming teaching series. Encourage your students to read the book of the Bible you will be studying.

- **Recap your main teaching points throughout the week.** Remind people of your sermon's main points by tweeting those ideas throughout the next week—one point every day or two. It will keep the sermon in front of your students and allow them to think about applying these truths in their everyday lives. This allows you to keep the conversation going.

communicating and connecting

- **Disciple people throughout the week.** Using social networking sites will allow you to disciple those in your ministry throughout the week. Share Scripture thoughts that are challenging you, or share a concept from an insightful book you're reading. This will give you an opportunity to be a shepherd throughout the week and pour into your ministry in new and innovative ways.

- **Share stories.** Let people know when your ministry was able to accomplish something amazing. Ask someone to write out their testimony of how they came to know Christ, or ask one of your leaders to share a little bit about their own life.

- **Recap mission trips or great events.** We use our ministry Facebook™ page to recap our retreats and large events. Facebook™ is a great way to post pictures and videos and tell stories of what God did at the retreat. People can comment on one another's pictures, and friendships will be strengthened as people reminisce about the time they had on the retreat.

effective discipleship

 Relationship is the foundation for discipleship.

Think of discipleship as mentoring. Without trust, it's impossible to have a healthy mentoring relationship. Without trust, the people you're mentoring will never open their hearts to listen to you or follow you. Reflect on the people who have had the greatest impact on you. It's likely they were people that you trusted, and you probably had deep, healthy relationships with them.

Before you start any formal discipleship "program," spend time getting to know the other person—and letting that person get to know you. Ask questions that will give you an opportunity to get to know a person's journey so far—highlights, struggles, spiritual growth, memories, and challenges. When you learn about someone's life experiences, you are doing two things. First, you learn how to communicate most effectively with that individual. Second, you build trust. Knowing each other's life stories is the cornerstone for building a strong relationship. Implementing this principle will help move from a teacher-to-student relationship toward a peer-to-peer relationship, which is an effective platform for discipleship.

Effective discipleship is more than just Bible study.

If you are a spiritual leader in the lives of students, then you have a desire to watch them grow closer to Jesus Christ. The process of becoming like Christ is what discipleship is all about. But how do we most effectively disciple people? Again, relationship must be the foundation. It is easy to miss this because too many Christians view discipleship as just a regimented structure of Scripture discussion and theological understanding.

My best discipleship moments happen when I intentionally involve people in my daily routines—in other words, doing whatever possible to "live life together." As leaders our call is to reveal to young people—as well as the adult leaders around us—how faith in Christ impacts everyday life. The most effective way to do this is to show them and not just tell them. When you need to run errands, call up one of the people you are connecting with and ask that person to join you. Find out what hobbies people have and join them in these activities. Moving discipleship relationships away from just coffee shops and church offices will give you fresh insight and greater opportunity to encourage application of the truths that you are discussing with your student.

113 Respect the spiritual journey of others.

As ministers and leaders we are called to lead and disciple people. One of the important things to consider is where people are in their spiritual journey before we disciple them. Keep in mind that discovering truths of the Lord is a journey people embark on, and you are a guide in someone's spiritual journey.

Discipleship relationships are based upon mutual respect, with a focus of spiritual growth. People mature differently, so as a leader you must allow others to figure out faith as they walk with God. Give them permission and opportunity to stumble along and process the truths of Jesus as you work with them. Asking questions will give you the best opportunity as a leader to discover where someone is spiritually and will provide insight into where and how to lead this person.

114 Intentionality enhances discipleship.

How much preparation do you put into your meetings with people you directly influence? Do you spend time thinking about where they are in their spiritual walk,

effective discipleship

and do you ask God for insight on ways you can more effectively challenge and encourage them? Taking just 10 minutes before meeting with a student will do wonders for the effectiveness of your time and effort. Obviously we are not talking about every conversation being scripted to the point of not having the freedom to freely talk about life. But think about these questions before you meet with someone:

- What Scriptures do you want this person to understand?

- In what areas of life could this person really use some insight about applying biblical truths?

- What principle do you want this person to grasp after your conversation?

- How do you see God working in this person's life right now?

Questions like these will give you a great foundation for the meeting you are going to have with this person. Being intentional about where you want to lead and guide this person spiritually will enhance the discipleship process greatly.

Don't replace the Holy Spirit in the discipleship process.

I have encountered many people in my life who were crucial to my spiritual growth. I learned major spiritual, life, and leadership principles from the time I spent with these men. As I look back at these leaders who influenced me, I remember times when they taught me candidly from the Scriptures and their life experiences. One thing I will always appreciate about these men is that they allowed the Holy Spirit to be my primary teacher.

Some leaders attempt discipleship by imparting their knowledge into the people they are mentoring. In some situations this may be important to do, but a leader's job isn't to replace the Holy Spirit. The Holy Spirit is promised to be our counselor, and he is much better at teaching through life situations than we are at imparting our knowledge. As you disciple people, teach them to listen to the Holy Spirit and assist them in seeing situations in which he wants to develop their life and ultimately their faith.

Spiritual change happens from the inside out.

How do you fully evaluate a person's spiritual maturity? How do you know if anything you're saying is even making a difference in the life of the person you're discipling? The answer: You often can't. When someone's hands are dirty and we put those hands under a faucet, we are able to see the dirt wash away and the hands become clean. Spiritually speaking we know that the work of Christ on the Cross cleanses people from the grime of the world. When we lead people spiritually and walk through the journey of discipleship with them, we can be confident that the work of the Holy Spirit in their life is doing things that we often cannot see.

Some trees remain dormant for years before they blossom. These trees are continually watered and nourished, yet year after year no visible physical changes occur—but they just *look* dead until finally blossoming to life. For reasons I don't understand, people can be the same way spiritually. We cannot evaluate the effectiveness of our discipleship in someone's life by that person's current behavior. In some people, spiritual fruit takes longer to blossom. Give them space and time to process and consider the things you're talking about. Resist the tendency to get them to conform to a certain pattern of behavior. Remember, the discipleship process progresses from the inside out, and behavior might be the last thing that changes—but that's OK.

Reconciliation is a life-changing theme to share with others.

"God blesses those who work for peace, for they will be called the children of God" (Matthew 5:9). As leaders, we have the responsibility to communicate truths and principles that Jesus lived out—and truths and principles we are called to emulate. The principle of reconciliation is a theme revealed through the ministry of Jesus in the Gospels. Broken relationships are prevalent in our culture today and greatly affect our students. Being a "peacemaker" in this world means encouraging peace and bringing together people who disagree or quarrel.

The idea of reconciliation does not solely focus on earthly relationships. We must be reconciled to the Father, and the work of Christ accomplished this. We can be leaders who encourage our students to share the light of Christ in the world by understanding and living out what the Bible communicates. Reconciliation is a major theme of Jesus Christ, and we would not be effectively discipling students if we did not teach this truth and show them how to live it out in their lives.

118 Teach people to love God before you send them out to love others.

Evangelism is one of the core purposes of the church as revealed in Scripture. We are called to be the light of the world, and this light must not be hidden—it should be set upon a hillside for all to see. Jesus himself said: *"Therefore, go and make disciples of all the nations, baptizing them in the name of the Father and the Son and the Holy Spirit" (Matthew 28:19).* We have come to know this as the Great Commission. However, as Christians, we often "go" with our spiritual cups totally empty. Many well-intentioned youth leaders send their students out into the world on short-term mission trips—or even into the "real world" after graduating from high school—without teaching one crucial principle of Jesus. Before Jesus communicated the Great Commission to his disciples, he shared something even more foundational. In Matthew 22, Jesus said that the greatest commandment was to love God with all your heart, soul, and mind. Then he said the second one is just like it: Love your neighbor as you love yourself.

As we disciple our students and share with them the call to be God's ambassadors in this world, we have the opportunity to communicate a truth that will fuel their passion for missions and evangelism for a lifetime. Loving God FIRST sounds so simple, yet it is easily overlooked in the excitement of going and doing missions and outreach.

Our heart for hurting people grows as our personal relationship with Jesus grows.

Your greatest mission field is the hearts of the students that you minister to each week. Teach them to love God first, then go out and impact the world.

impacting people

119 Bus drivers and taxi cab drivers take people where they know they want to go; leaders take them places they didn't know they could go.

The role of leaders is to inspire and lead people to places they never thought they could go. As a God-designed leader, you have the privilege of accurately evaluating the current reality and leading people to realities that will benefit them spiritually. People typically limit themselves and allow their current circumstances to dictate where they go in life, but leaders move them forward and help them see a different reality. Conformity is a common struggle. Some people naturally stretch the imagination of others, but oftentimes there is a limit to where people believe they can go.

Leaders don't just help people stretch their current reality; they help people see a whole new reality. This takes a long time, and the process of helping people see something different for themselves is never an easy one. Be prepared for challenges and pushback. However, be a leader that isn't afraid to guide people to places they will probably resist—reveal to them the benefits of moving to the place you foresee.

Care for people more than programs.

What do you do as a leader when a volunteer or student doesn't follow through with a responsibility? Do you get angry, or should you let it go and chalk it up to something that just happens in ministry? As a leader it is easy to get frustrated at someone who doesn't follow through because we have ministries that are based on putting on a program—weekly services, retreat, social events, and so on. No matter how big of a mistake someone makes, I want to encourage you to value the person who didn't follow through more than the program that didn't go the way it was planned. Programs come and go, and most times the crowd won't even know things didn't go as planned.

On the other hand, if we get overly frustrated at someone for a mistake, we risk the potential of creating bigger problems. Let's agree to be leaders who shepherd our flocks by looking for teachable moments that will help others see areas of improvement in their lives and encourage them to continue to walk with God. This is what it means to focus your ministry on relationships rather than results.

121 Relationship is the baseline for every good leader.

An effective leader supplies what people need and finds out about people through healthy relationships. If you cannot build relationships with people, then you cannot lead them effectively. Leaders who are focused on getting the work done apart from relationships are not leading people—they are managing work. The most effective leaders are able to connect with people, encourage them, and lead them within the context of healthy relationships. That's how we are able to get to know someone personally, and when we get to know the core of a person we are then able to lead that person more effectively because core needs will be revealed. You will never be able to supply what people need without getting to know them.

122 Seek honest, wise, experience-soaked answers—not just what you want to hear.

It's easy for leaders to listen to the people that will agree with us and view those who oppose our thoughts as people who just "don't get it." Effective leaders listen to the advice of godly people who believe in them and believe in what

impacting people

God is doing within their ministry. Think about your church or ministry setting. What people can you surround yourself with to help you make strategic decisions?

One suggestion would be to find people about 15-20 years older than you to help you see things coming down the road in your life that you may not see right now. These don't have to be pastors or church leaders—in fact, they probably shouldn't be! Get some outside perspective. People with greater wisdom and life experience will often be more honest about circumstances than those that are closer to your age. After prayerfully including these advisers in your leadership circle, trust them and listen to what they have to say. You don't have to follow through with every suggestion or thought they give you, but be open to considering the advice of others.

Don't assume anything—when making a big decision get as many opinions as possible.

One major mistake leaders make is assuming they know what's best for the groups they lead. You are the leader because you have demonstrated an ability to lead people, inspire them, and set a course for the future. But don't allow this opportunity to deceive you into thinking that you have all the answers. No one is able to make consistently effective decisions alone. Getting the perspective of other people will help you see things that you wouldn't have seen otherwise.

I am a very visionary person, and if I'm not careful, I have a tendency to make a decision and move forward without thinking of the details and consequences. One of my team members is very administratively gifted, so before I move forward on any idea or new vision for ministry, I run the idea past her. She does a great job of showing me potential pitfalls and giving me thoughts on how to communicate this new vision clearly. Talk with people within your ministry before you make a major decision or shift, and you'll get perspectives from people who will be affected—and you will most likely get ideas that you wouldn't have thought of on your own. Still, at the end of the day, you're a leader who's called to make a decision. Just don't make it alone.

Don't study counterfeits—study the real thing.

When government officials try to catch counterfeit currency, they don't study forgery; they simply know what the real thing looks like. If you are familiar with the real thing, then you will be able to spot inaccuracies in an instant. The same holds true for leaders that lead Christian ministry. Study models and methods of ministry that have withstood the test of time so you can better evaluate all you are doing to impact people. There is great wisdom in studying Christian movements in history that have been highly successful at sharing the love of God and leaving a lasting imprint in the world. In our day of technology we are able to communicate with leaders all over the globe, so research what others are doing to be effective for the kingdom. If you take the time to consider methods, systems, and programs that have been successful in other places, you will find yourself coming up with creative ways to implement the principles you see as you lead others. As you take a look at successful ministry strategies you will gain insight on potential pitfalls in your own ministry strategy.

 Be a hope giver.

As we look out the windows of our churches, from the porches of our homes, and toward the individuals on the television screen, we see a world that has lost hope. As Christian leaders we are called to minister to a world that has lost hope. The hope we share is not of this world; it's a supernatural hope that is the only thing that can fulfill people. As I interact with students I do my best to point them toward the hope of a relationship with Jesus Christ. There is no other message that comes close to the work of Christ on the Cross. This is a hope that changes a person's heart. People are looking for hope in this world, and those who don't believe in God have not just given up on God—they have given up on hope.

When you put together messages or meet with that friend who is struggling in life, remember that the words Jesus spoke in the Bible were intended to lead people to the Father. Communicating the eternal hope found in relationship with the Father is our call as leaders and ministers. May we never forget that we are hope planters, and may we take seriously the call to share this good news with a world that has lost hope.

126 Christian leadership points people toward Jesus, not ourselves.

There is this incredible passage in the book of John when John's disciples see Jesus for the first time (John 1:35-37). This short passage of Scripture says a lot about John's leadership and humility. John sees Jesus and points out the Messiah to his disciples. They immediately start following Jesus.

This may not sound like a big deal, but in the heart of a leader this truth is vital. It is easy for us to build our own kingdoms and desire recognition and admiration from the people we lead. However, our mission is to tell people about Jesus and inspire them to follow him—not us—for the rest of their lives. There are many ministries whose identities rest upon the personality of the leader.

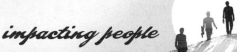

impacting people

John modeled great leadership with his own disciples. It is almost as if they said to themselves, "Look, it's the one John told us about. All this time we were with him, he told us about this Messiah and now he is before our eyes. Let's follow him like John told us to." There is no better satisfaction than leading people to Jesus and watching them follow him.

Who are the people you have been given influence over? Whom do they follow? If your students saw Jesus, would they recognize him and would they immediately follow him? Our leadership has the ability to help people shape a worldview filled with a hunger to meet the Messiah and an eagerness to follow him.

 ## Expose yourself to different situations to encounter unexpected ministry opportunities.

One common trap for pastors and ministry leaders is to get so involved in the work of ministry that we forget the "outside world." If we can interact with different groups of people, we can discover a plethora of opportunities to creatively share God's love. I suggest you find ways to connect with segments of your local community that you usually wouldn't see. Meet business leaders and city employees in your community. Doing your sermon prep at a coffee shop or taking a walk through a crowded part of town during the workweek will ensure that you meet new people. Look at the local community calendar and see what events are coming though your city. Take some time to go places that you normally wouldn't visit.

Our community has a leadership program for young professionals. I signed up for the program, and for nine months I gathered with young professionals from around the community. I was able to engage in some very fascinating conversations. Most of these people were from the business community and could not understand why a pastor would participate in this program. However, the conversations and time I was able to invest in these relationships helped me make an impact in the lives of these men and women. I suggest you get involved in your community and live out the mission of Christ outside the walls of the church. You never know what kind of opportunities the Holy Spirit will reveal as you enter the marketplace of your community